TELESFORO RODRIGUEZ

Guest curator/essayist

Marta Turok

Presidente

Asociacion Mexicana de Arte y Cultura Popular, A.C.

with text and essay by

Annie O'Neill

artist/collector and former advisor to the

Nelson A Rockefeller Mexican Folk Art Collection

Marijo Dougherty

Project Director

Living Traditions
Mexican Popular Arts

September 15 through November 22, 1992

Organized by the University Art Museum

University at Albany

State University of New York

Living Traditions
Mexican Popular Arts

© Copyright 1992
University at Albany
State University of New York
All Rights Reserved

Exhibition and Catalog designed by Zheng Hu
Text was set in Adobe® Goudy Old Style (text) and Palatino (cover) and page layout on Ventura Publisher/GEM®. Film output on a Linotronic Imagesetter. Three thousand copies of this catalog were printed and bound by Brodock Press Inc., Utica, New York on Mohawk Innovation #100 text and #80 cover.

Photographs by Gary Gold
Additional photographs by Lee Boltin, plates 19, 45 and 59, courtesy of Ann Rockefeller Roberts.

Library of Congress Catalog Card Number: 92-062384
ISBN: 0-910763-07-0

This publication is made possible by a grant from the Fideicomiso para la Cultura Mexico-Estados Unidos, with additional support from the Office of the President, University at Albany and the Mexican Cultural Institute of New York.

Cover: Plate 64
Selected Figures from Heaven and Hell Installation, University Art Museum, 1992. Carved bull and devils by Manuel Jiménez.

Frontispiece: Plate 40
Telesforo Rodriguez (Ameyaltepec, Guerrero), *Fiesta*,
ca. 1975, bark painting, 32 x 46 inches.

All works included in the exhibition, unless otherwise noted, are from the collection of Annie O'Neill.

Table of Contents

FOREWORD

    H. Patrick Swygert 7

    The Honorable Manuel Alonso 8

ESSAY

    Survival Through Change: A Look at Mexican
    Popular Arts on the Eve of the Twenty-First Century
    Marta Turok 10

    The Artisans and Markets of Mexico:
    A Collector's View
    Annie O'Neill 29

EXHIBITION SCRIPT

    Introduction 41

    Home and Hearth/Hogar y Fogon 42

    Innovators/Innovadores 54

    Popular Arts in Transition
    El Arte Popular en Transicion 64

    Ceremonial Objects/Objetos Ceremoniales 76

ACKNOWLEDGMENTS 84

Exhibition Overview, University Art Museum, September 1992

Foreword

Living Traditions: Mexican Popular Arts, an exhibition that the University at Albany's Art Museum is privileged to present, is a fiesta with many, many celebrants.

This fiesta is the harvest of months of collaborative efforts between the Mexican Cultural Institute of New York and the University at Albany. Manuel Alonso, Consul General of Mexico, and Mireya Terán, Executive Director of the Mexican Cultural Institute of New York, provided financial support and intellectual guidance. The exhibition simply could not have been mounted without Consul General Alonso's help.

We celebrate as well the generosity of Annie O'Neill for sharing her treasures with the thousands who will learn, many for the first time, of some of the richness of Mexican folk art. We also thank Mr. and Mrs. Eugene Walter and Pilar Gomez for lending additional objects which enhance the exhibition further. We thank as well Marta Turok, Guest Curator of the exhibition, an internationally renowned scholar who has helped in ways too numerous to recite. Marijo Dougherty, Associate Director of the University at Albany Art Museum, and Zheng Hu, Exhibits Designer, labored longer than any to bring this vision to reality. Sponsors and volunteers, students and faculty, and Nancy Liddle, Director of the Art Museum, all warrant our thanks.

Ultimately, this fiesta celebrates the artists, known and unknown, whose work we exhibit. The range of expression one encounters, from the *Day of the Dead* exhibit area to the contemporary weavings of Isaac Vasquez, conveys the passion of the artists. In doing so, it moves us as well. The fanciful and grotesque, the objects of utility, and the images of the artists' daily reality singly and together touch the viewer. There is an exuberance throughout. And not simply the exuberance of the innocent village. The city is here as well. All of Mexico comes together in this exhibition. And all of us can join in the fiesta.

H. Patrick Swygert
President
University at Albany
State University of New York

The richness in creativity and imagination of the Mexican people, and most of all their passion to preserve their traditions, have given the world a whole universe of beauty and color in popular art. Originating within the context of magical and ceremonial cultures, popular art in my country not only belongs to the individuals who create it; it changes and at the same time remains unchanged, and finally it belongs to the whole community. The humble people of my country, peasants and those who use their hands to till the soil, vest this same love for their labor into beautiful pieces of ceramic, textiles, colorful toys, wood carvings, jewelry, and even in the making of breads, candies and everyday tortillas.

The making of popular art is a tradition but new forms and ideas are reinvented continually. This process takes place in the cities as well, where contemporary modern images and materials are incorporated into the marketplaces, the fiestas, music, song, and performances. The vitality of these art forms testify to the pride and love with which Mexicans keep the creative spirit of their ancestors alive.

We at the Mexican Consulate in New York and at the Mexican Cultural Institute, have been closely committed to the University at Albany to make this project a reality. Whatever we were able to accomplish, was thanks to the personal interest of H. Patrick Swygert, President of the University at Albany, who enabled the Mexican program of activities to take place. We acknowledge the dedication, creativity and great effort of our friend Marijo Dougherty and the staff at the Museum. We have learned a lot from her work and decisions, and we admire the role she played in this Mexican/American collaboration.

On the Mexican side, we were very pleased to have Marta Turok, President of the Mexican Association of Art and Popular Culture, a Mexican citizen, as the guest curator of the exhibition. She has impeccable and prestigious credentials both in Mexico and abroad and we are indeed fortunate that she agreed to undertake this project.

We also received invaluable support from many Mexican institutions: The Ministry of Foreign Affairs, the Ministry of Tourism, the Government of the State of Hidalgo, the Fondo Nacional para la Cultura y las Artes, and Mexicana Airlines. We are also grateful to the Fideicomiso para la Cultura Mexico-Estados Unidos for awarding a grant which makes possible this catalog for the exhibition.

Manuel Alonso
Cónsul General de México
Chairman of the Board, Mexican Cultural Institute of New York

La riqueza creativa e imaginativa del pueblo mexicano, y ante todo su pasión por preservar sus tradiciones, han dado al mundo todo un universo de belleza y color en sus artes populares. El arte popular de mi país tiene su origen en un contexto cultural mágico y ceremonial, donde el objeto no tan sólo pertenece a aquél que lo crea, sino que al cambiar y al mismo tiempo permanecer intacto, llega a ser parte de toda la comunidad donde nace.

La gente humilde de mi país los campesinos y todas aquellos que trabajan la tierra con las manos, plasman ese mismo amor con que labran los surcos en el campo en la creación de hermosas piezas de cerámica, textiles, coloridos juguetes, tallas en madera, joyeria y aun panes, dulces y las mismas tortillas del alimento cotidíano.

La confección de arte popular es una tradición muy nuestra, sin embargo, se reinventan continuamente ideas y formas nuevas. De esta manera el proceso llega hasta los grandes centros urbanos donde se absorbe esta tradición y donde nos encontramos con una multitud de imágenes y materiales modernos y contemporáneos en mercados y fiestas, en la música, la danza y en infinidad de representaciones populares. La vitalidad de esta forma artística es testimonio del legítimo orgullo y del amor con que los mexicanos mantienen latente el espíritu creativo de sus antepasados.

El Consulado General de México en Nueva York y el Instituto Cultural Mexicano se identificaron plenamente con la Universidad de Albany para que este proyecto se hiciera realidad. Cualquier logro que contenga esta exposición se debe merced al interés personal del señor H. Patrick Swygert, Presidente de la Universidad en Albany, del Estado de Nueva York, quien apoyó la presentación del programa de actividades que acompañan la exposición. Asimismo queremos reconocer la dedicación, la creatividad y el gran empeño de nuestra buena amiga Marijó Dougherty y de su equipo de colaboradores en el Museo. Hemos aprendido mucho de sus decisiones y de su trabajo, y al mismo tiempo admiramos el papel que Marijó ha desempeñado en esta colaboración México-Estados Unidos.

Por parte de México, nada nos complace más que haber tenido la aportación de Marta Turok, Presidente de la Asociación Mexicana de Arte y Cultura Popular, como curadora invitada de la exhibición. Marta Turok posee un prestigio profesional impecable, tanto en México como en el extranjero, por lo que nos sentimos afortunados de su contribución a este proyecto.

Hemos también recibido apoyo invaluable de diversas instituciones mexicanas; la Secretaría de Relaciones Exteriores, la Secretaría de Turismo, el Gobierno del Estado de Hidalgo, el Fondo Nacional para la Cultura y las Artes y Mexicana de Aviación. Justo es expresar también nuestro reconocimiento al Fideicomiso para la Cultura México-Estados Unidos por habernos otorgado el subsidio que hizo posible la publicación del catálogo que enriquece esta exposición.

Manuel Alonso
Cónsul General de México
Presidente del Consejo del Instituto Cultural Mexicano de Nueva York

Survival Through Change: A Look at Mexican Popular Arts on the Eve of the Twenty-First Century

The Multiple Facets of Mexican Popular Arts

The study of popular arts in Mexico is a fascinating, yet equally complex field. Our popular arts are like a window through which one can visualize and embody the microcosm of an entire social fabric. Many factors come into play, and this art form is probably the longest lasting expression in the rise and development of culture.

We may envision the universal aspects of culture as three concentric circles, with the popular arts connecting all three. In the first circle is the satisfaction of our basic needs for food, shelter and protection. This ensures the reproduction and conservation of our species. The objects and tools invented and developed for this purpose, through our daily contact with nature, constitute our material culture. The second circle contains the multiple ways in which we organize in social units allowing us to best fulfill these needs. The roles men, women, children, and elders play indicate the amount of tasks which must be performed, and the degree of social institutions that have been created. The third circle contains the ingredients essential to nourish our spirit and culture through religion, art and a cosmogony of symbols. In these we delve for our origins, fill our lives with meaning through ceremonies and rituals, and embellish the objects that surround us.

The raw materials employed to create these objects of material culture point to the profound relationship between society and nature, as each group discovers and transforms the available and useful plant, mineral, and animal resources. The value of culture in this relationship is that knowledge is built upon generation after generation, where each group (under normal conditions) exercises self-control to assure the sustainability of their resources. Scornfully considered *empirical* knowledge by the scientific world, as Ethnoscience, it is a body of applied knowledge, with rules and logic of its own, that can offer many choices towards sustainable development in the wake of ecological disasters.

The development of technology and industry is also related, for it is in this sphere that each group fulfills their productive potential based on their organizational capacity and technological expertise. Among hunters and gatherers, for example, each family or unit has to make the baskets, ropes, spears and skins it requires. On the other hand, among sedentary groups, specialization occurs. This, in fact, constitutes the beginning of industry, and of barter and exchange.

The relationship between technology and design is probably one of the most underrated aspects

Plate 1, Clay water jug, Amate, 15 x 8 x 8 inches

in the Popular Arts. If we take a closer look at the connection between form and function, water-jugs are probably one of the best examples (Plate 1). Throughout the world, for thousands of years, elementary principles of physics have been applied to water-jugs, resulting in four basic design elements. The nature of the problem requires that a liquid be retrieved from a distance, and transported either by animal or human means; liquid set in motion has a rate of displacement double the movement it is subject to. What are the possible solutions? The result is a small, flat base, a large round "stomach", a narrow tapered "mouth", and two or three "ears" at the sides to ease lifting and storage. Once these conditions are met, however, hundreds of interpretations exist just of this one form. One must conclude that it is in designs and decorations applied to utilitarian objects where culture and identity express themselves.

Art and aesthetics are probably the elements one associates most with the cultural dimension of Mexican Popular Arts, but they certainly are not the only ones. More often than not, these artistic aspects are a masterful blend of culture, environment and technology. The added ingredient that makes a profound difference in the visual impact is cosmogony, the highly abstract and symbolic element of mythic thought that explains how each group orders and defines their vision of the universe—earth, the firmament and the underworld. In this realm, forms and designs are like semantic units loaded with meaning. A votive arrow is a symbol of communication between people and deities; it might differ slightly in form from a normal hunting arrow by the type of feathers attached, by the abstract designs painted on it, or by its size; but it definitely differs in its function—which is entirely symbolic. Though the role of symbolism is best represented in ceremonial and ritual artifacts (Plate 58), it doesn't exclude utilitarian wares and the way they are decorated. Quite the contrary, aesthetic codes are the sum of the basic units of design—abstract or not—that are combined and recombined in such a fashion that a distinctive, identifiable, cultural style emerges (Plate 4).

Mexico's extraordinary biological diversity has gone hand in hand with its cultural diversity. Long before the Spanish Invasion, at least 100 distinct ethnic groups with their languages, philosophies and cultures inhabited our Nation. And 500 years later, 56 groups still exercise their rights to practice the culture that has resulted from centuries of oppression and poverty. Numerically, they are the most important producers of Ethnic and Popular Arts.

Economic factors are also involved in the popular arts. Here production costs, labor and time, prices, markets and marketing come to the foreground. In a *natural economy*, the material culture objects produced within the community circulate internally; their use-value has no monetary consequences, though economic categories of cost, time invested and labor incorporated are implicit. That culture isn't quantifying, it doesn't matter if a ceremonial garment took over a year to weave, and the finest raw materials were used, because it is not meant to be sold (Plate 20).

On the other hand, in a *mercantile economy*, goods acquire value as commodities to be exchanged in a market, based on the comparative labor each object represents (Plate 56). Pricing, the laws of supply and demand, and bartering (or haggling), become essential tools the producer learns to handle. In *capitalism*, new elements are incorporated, as workshops and factories transform the whole productive system. Through the introduction of private ownership of the means of production and the existence of hired workers, the division of labor that takes place enables the owner to add value to his investment.

Historically in Mexico (especially during the last few decades), ethnic groups whose material

Plate 2, **Angel Cruz** (Tecomatepec, Mexico), *Pulque Pitcher*, 14 x 10 1/2 x 11 inches.

culture was exclusively a part of the *natural* economy, have been thrust into a *market* economy without the experience and conceptual tools they need to avoid being exploited. More recently, both mercantile and self-consumption groups have found that due to *their* precarious income situation, a third, unrelated party, takes over and sub-contracts the output through piece-work, giving ethnic groups the raw materials and paying a pittance for their labor.

Another development is the division among artisans into a clear-cut socioeconomic pyramid: five percent are at the peak, and are usually the great *innovators* (who now run workshops and/or stores, aside from their commission work), or astute craftsmen who engage in wholesale commercial sale of crafts, buying cheaply from the poorer craftspeople; thirty-five percent are making inexpensive *copies* of the innovators work, and perhaps combining this production with traditional crafts. The remaining sixty percent eke out a living by producing everyday utilitarian wares, or worse, selling their artistic labor to more successful workshops. *These artisans are obviously the most vulnerable sector.*

This takes us to our last point—that culture is, and always has been, by its nature, dynamic. Therefore, it is imperative to look at the processes of *change*, no matter what time frame one is observing. Once again, one must engage in cross-reference with the cultural, the cosmogonic, the environmental, the technological, the artistic, and the economic. As one looks into the last few decades, one must also add new marketing strategies, and the role of governments, official and private agencies and individuals. Change can be exciting, a whole new world of opportunities to innovate. Change can also be violent if total substitution, loss, and destruction takes place.

In the world of popular arts, one of the major issues is who is in control of the situation? Are the vital artistic and aesthetic decision-making processes still in the hands of the artisan/popular artist, or have governments, official and/or private agencies and individuals given them a specific pattern to repeat exactly and continuously?

Fortunately Mexican Popular Arts are provocative—they are not an objective and cold field of study. They are charged with a premeditated subjectivity that gives them that rare quality of turning the most arrogant observer into a humbled soul. This reaction is produced by contact with the central protagonists in this process—the artisans. It would be difficult not to believe that anyone who has actively participated in the popular arts has not asked oneself a thousand times "What is it in this austere work environment, with such simple materials and tools, that makes it possible for the creation of such technically complex objects; objects so harmonious in their design and form yet so subtly different each one from the other, *even within the same village?*" And, they can differ radically from one neighboring culture to another!

Although definitions in this field are deemed dangerous, in my 1988 book *Como Acercarse a la Artesania* (How to Approach Crafts), I state "an artisan's greatest difference from a production worker is that the artisan still maintains a complete vertical and integral connection with each and every phase of production, beginning with the selection of his/her raw materials and ending with the final aesthetic decision. This very fact is also a clue to understanding how the creative and artistic dimensions of popular arts are born of the intimate and symbiotic relationship established between discipline and skill, between that which is earthly and that which is mythic, that is, the fusion of the corporal with the spiritual."

Those of us who have promoted these arts also know how unjust contemporary history has been to artisans and their craft. I think that many of us have felt powerless more than once when viewing the magnitude of the necessities of the artisans juxtaposed with the general magnitude of their poverty. The majority of artisans depend upon middlemen and loansharks who in each region play the role of a "necessary evil" in the process.

How many times in the popular arts have we seen or relived together the old story of the Conquistadores bartering glass beads for gold, yet today, creativity and work are still exchanged for a few coins or a few cups of alcohol. Is the modern curse of the popular arts always to be the sacrifice of the value of one's work when faced with the "competitive" market price? When will these so-called "minor arts" stop being relegated to an inferior status and undervalued by art history? As a result of all of this, each path that one chooses to make in order to aid and spread the knowledge of the popular arts has its degree of validity; every grain of sand lends itself to global solutions.

The (Re) Discoveries
Curiously enough, we as Americans and Mexicans have coalesced in the same space as a result of two different sets of roots and histories of rediscovery. Up until the advent of the Industrial Revolution,

crafts were the only industrial form that existed. When machines replaced them, new terms began to appear to distinguish them, such as "manual industries", "decorative arts" or "applied arts". Their predicted inevitable demise and disappearance at the hands of the "cursed mechanization" that was occurring, was counteracted by the rise of the Arts and Crafts Movement in England, which exalted distinctive articles with the stamp, "handmade". For very different reasons, at the beginning of the Twentieth Century, nascent states such as Mexico, with a significant peasant population, looked for symbols that would help groups, separated socially and economically from one another for centuries, to identify culturally with each other and to unite.

The term Popular Arts is born in Mexico through the praising of the *mestizo*—the descendents created from the fusion formed through Cortés and his Indian lover, la Malinche, as opposed to the *criollo*—the son/daughter born in Mexico of Spanish parents. The *mestizo* was extolled for his intrinsic qualities, for his sensitive soul, for his creative spirit descendent from an anonymous people who embellished utilitarian objects by necessity. These popular arts lived an ephemeral moment of glory together with early Muralism. Famous artists, such as Diego Rivera, Frida Kahlo, Dr. Atl (Gerardo Murillo), Roberto Montenegro and Miguel Covarrubias collected them, painted them and promoted them. They in turn influenced Americans such as William Spratling, Donald and Dorothy Cordry and René d'Harnoncourt who passed through the most remote villages on foot, horse or mule in order to document these arts and form private or museum collections in the face of the impending threat of their disappearance.

Today, on the eve of the Twenty-First Century, we know that their dire predictions did not come true. Crafts and the popular arts remain alive, and on firm ground both in industrial societies and in those societies still on the road to "modern" development. But, and it is a great *but*, "Have all of them survived?" "Have they survived in the same form?" One must examine the situation case by case, because there are crafts that have in fact completely disappeared (such as the incredible cochineal-dyed traditional skirts from the Oaxaca Valley). There are communities who have forsaken craft production altogether due to changing consumer buying patterns and/or other job opportunities. There are still crafts in nearby villages such as Teotitlán del Valle and Santa Ana del Valle where textile activity not only flourishes but involves many more families in craft activities than forty years ago. At the same time, in new and traditional markets alike, one can still find sections specializing in utilitarian pottery, baskets, mats and carved stone *metates* and *molcajetes* (mortar and pestle grinder) which have a production history of hundreds and even thousands of years (Plate 3).

An initial interest in the popular arts, I found, can expand into a lifetime involvement. Throughout the last twenty years the question of survival of popular art has guided me in my travels, in my studies, and in my work. At the end of 1991 I visited the collection of Annie O'Neill, housed in her home in upstate, New York. My aim was to define the focus of the exhibit *Living Traditions: Mexican Popular Arts* which was largely drawn from her collection. I not only identified with the pieces I saw but also with her. Without personally knowing one another, we had been graced to live through the same epoch. We shared a similar vision: understanding that change and continuity could range from *imperceptible* alterations to *grand transformations* in the popular arts of Mexico. Our mutual desire was to convey the message that the vortex of changes are not endangering traditions, but rather that the ensuing iconography has enriched the visual representations of their culture.

The best way to explain change would be to delve into the roots, to retrace the steps of the community and the popular artist, and to try to reconstruct the links between them. How was a particular object used by the culture that needed it? How did the artisan respond to this need? What were the traceable stylistic variations and their possible origins? How did they contribute to reconstructing the puzzle? Annie O'Neill's collection offered very good examples of timeless material culture that could be placed in the exhibition into two basic categories:

> 1. Pieces whose main function is utilitarian and used in the home, in the kitchen, or as clothing. This broad section, which we named *Home and Hearth*, symbolizes a woman's place, and historically her means of creativity (Plate 10).

> 2. Works which have been created for ceremonial and religious purposes. These were included in a section we named *Ceremonial Folk Art: Form and Symbol*. Ex-votos, retablos, angels, incense burners, candelabra, masks, ceremonial clothing, figures used for the *Day of the Dead* celebration, objects for home altars (Plate 13), and various indigenous votive offerings were included. Other objects included in this section were masks, lent by Mr. and Mrs. Eugene Walter (Plate 42), and indigenous dance costumes, lent by Pilar Gomez (Plate 41).

Change is best illustrated by showing sequences, with examples of as many transitional styles as possible. Annie O'Neill's collection had two interesting categories which showed change: one which illustrated when a broader community-based change took place (the Amate-paper painters from Guerrero (Plate 39), the Huichol Indians (Plate 54), the potters from Ocumicho, the lacquer producers of Olinalá and Temalacazingo)(Plate 14), and the other, which illustrated clearly defined *Innovators* who had created a mini-Revolution in their midst. This section would include work by Heron Martinez, Teodora Blanco, Josefina Aguilar, Aurelio Flores, Pedro Linares, Saulo Moreno, Isaac Vasquez.

Thus, the broad category *"Popular Arts in Transition: New Art Forms and Old Traditions"* highlights a phenomena that was occurring in various parts of Mexico beginning in the 1920s, although it intensified in the post-war period of the 1950s. In the contemporary artisan world, the three elements of culture, economics and innovation all interact. Cultural goods are converted into commodities which then leave their local and regional realms and begin a new trail towards the homes of cosmopolitan inhabitants of the industrialized world. In this process the artisan confronts the necessity of having to constantly innovate and adapt to the needs and tastes of the new consumer without losing his/her cultural foundations.

An Era of Transformations
It has always been insisted that crafts are a complementary activity to agricultural production. One of the changes that I have detected is the reverse: *the agricultural production has become the complementary activity in numerous artisan communities*. The available amount of cultivatable land has been reduced and crafts have become a more lucrative enterprise. No matter how small their plots are, the artisan never loses contact with the soil, the cosmos, or with the cultivation of maize. It has also been possible to

observe that religious ties have been conserved through the artisans' participation in the cycle of village *fiestas*; they still want to continue living in their communities. We now have a certain security that the cultural foundations will continue to maintain themselves, although their outward manifestations will change.

The next question is "Why do the manifestations change?" The response is that everything begins to change through the intervention of the consumer and through the change in the profile of this consumer, the person who acquires the objects. Everyday, the more handmade utilitarian rural objects are displaced by industrially manufactured ones, which can be sold at a lower price. Artisans must decide if they should abandon their activities, or find new and alternative markets for their goods. Historically, the artisan that made a water jug, a pitcher or a vase to sell in the market, also used the object. This permitted the continual purification and perfection of the design. Now, the artisan is asked to make coffee pots and dinnerware sets that he/she will never use and are not subject to the continual streamlining process, requiring outside technical aid to target design problems. Artisans, in order to survive, have sometimes made adaptations to please the customs of modern, urban people. Since this is not a mechanical or automatic process, it is fascinating to try to establish the sequence of adaptation that a particular artisan or an entire community have followed as they come up with novel solutions to the problems.

After re-reading Dr. Atl's book *The Popular Arts of Mexico* (published in 1921), the sixth chapter on "The Tendencies of Transformation" drew my attention because a part of it categorically affirmed that "the indigenous industries cannot transform themselves nor improve themselves: they are what they are." Yet, in another part of the same chapter he summarizes an experience in Tonalá, Jalisco in 1915, when an outsider had ordered some ceramic pitchers to be made in a manner distinct from the local style, asking that Aztec and Toltec fretwork be incorporated in the design. In the author's opinion, the result was catastrophic as the pottery completely lost its character. He continues:

> "The artistic instinct of the decorators of Tonalá caused them to mediate little by little the imposition of this fretwork and to extract and apply those Aztec, Toltec or Maya archaeological elements that fit in with their own artistic sensitivities. They began to apply them in a more restrained fashion to the antique designs and new shapes of their fired pottery."

This reaffirms something I have observed: for an innovation to meld harmoniously there must exist a *transition* period where not only does the artisan become familiar with the new shapes, conceptions and drawings, but filters what is superfluous and places his/her own seal on the work once the new process is appropriated. It is important to continue to document this process of change that has taken place in crafts since the 1950s, and attempt to establish the reasons behind these changes in order to perceive stylistic evolutions. Whether creativity and aesthetics enter into contradiction with market demands through outsiders' thematic suggestions, is an unanswered question. Doubt also arises whether over-recognition of individual talents is detrimental to the collective fountain of inspiration.

How do these changes express themselves?

What marks the history of these popular arts throughout the centuries, perhaps millennia, is their *functionality*: they were created as utilitarian objects for the home or they had liturgical, ceremonial and/or ritual object use. The existence of the *decorative arts* is not a cut and dried subject. The great transformation during this century has been the emergence of a figurative popular arts, almost statuesque in its form, increasingly baroque in its style, made to be seen and not necessarily used (Plate 25). In addition, behind every innovation and innovator there exists an object or cultural concept at its foundation: behind the Huichol yarn painting is the *nearica* or votive gourd (Plate 55); the painted water jugs were the antecedent for the amate paintings (Plate 36); the incense burners and *sahumerios* have been converted into dolls and *Trees of Life* (Plate 27); the whistles, on many occasions used by the shamans, (not as toys as they have been historically described to us), have been converted into lascivious devils; and upon prohibiting the burning of the gigantic Judas figures during Holy Week, over a ten year period they sprang horns and wings, their size was reduced and the *alebriges* were born (Plate 29).

We are filled with optimism over the creativity and genius of the popular artisan, yet there are problems in their future. The commercial success of popular arts and crafts goes hand in hand with the exploitation of raw materials, leading to an imminent ecological disaster. The lack of parallel environment protection and re-forestation programs for the various species of trees that the artisans need and use extensively (the amate, linaloe, copal and ironwood, canes, palms and agaves, among others), needs to be a priority. Artisans must also deal with modern knowledge concerning health hazards. Potters utilizing lead glaze in their work must now conform with new regulations regarding its usage. The exorbitant cost of this technological upgrade is prohibitive for most; in addition they must deal with the diminishing availability of firewood for use in their kilns. The end result is that production of the most traditional mole *cazuela* and *frijoles* pot used in the culture for centuries is now endangered.

As collectors, promoters, merchants, public servants and researchers we have interacted with the artisans, suggesting new themes to them, motivating the best and most creative among them commissioning works as *Patrons of the Arts*, putting together exhibitions, organizing competitions that award technical excellence, innovation and/or traditional forms. We have a responsibility to highlight their achievements, to celebrate them, to support them. It was a great victory in 1984 to achieve the inclusion of the category of *Arts and Popular Traditions* as part of the National Award for the Arts and Sciences in Mexico. This award is the highest honor that the nation bestows in the arts, and the only category open to communities, groups and to individuals, in recognition of the collective basis of popular creativity. Fortunately, it has been, is, and will be the artisans who have the last word. Their work speaks for them and for my country.

Marta Turok
Guest Curator

Curator's Note: There is no doubt in my mind that this exhibit would not have been possible without Marijo Dougherty's indomitable spirit. She just wouldn't take no for an answer on anything, and probably part of the reason had to do with the enthusiastic response and total commitment H. Patrick Swygert, President of the University at Albany, has given this project. Thanks to Zheng Hu for dealing with Mexican baroqueness in its clash with Oriental simplicity, to Joanne Lue for her ever-ready smile and to Gary Gossen of the University at Albany Anthropology Department for recommending me as guest curator. My most sincere acknowledgement to Consul General Manuel Alonso and Mireya Terán from the Mexican Cultural Institute of New York for their continued support, and to the Fideicomiso para la Cultura Mexico-Estados Unidos that has made this catalog possible.

Plate 3, *Molcajete* (Cuanjo, Michoacán), volcanic rock, 5 x 7 1/2 x 7 inches.

Plate 4, *Pitcher* (Atzompa, Oaxaca) *with Chocolate Beaters* (San Antonio la Isla, Mexico), 9 x 7 3/4 with 12 inch carved wooden beaters. On loan from Marta Turok.

Sobrevivencia a Través del Cambio: Una Mirada a las Artes Populares de México en los Albores del Siglo XXI

Los Contextos del Arte Popular Mexicano

Lo que hace que el estudio y el acercamiento al campo del arte popular en México resulte tan fascinante y, a la vez, tan complejo, es que nuestro Arte Popular es como una ventanita por la que uno puede visualizar y abarcar el microcosmos de todo un tejido social. Numerosos factores intervienen, y las artes populares seguramente constituyen el eslabón mas antiguo entre la evolución de la especie humana y el surgimiento y desarrollo de la cultura.

Incluso me atreveré a sugerir que las artes populares interactúan con los aspectos universales de la cultura, mismos que podemos sintetizar a través de tres esferas concéntricas.

En la primer esfera entra la conservación y reproducción de la especie, a través de la satisfacción de sus requerimientos de alimentación, refugio y abrigo. Objetos y herramientas son inventados y desarrollados a través del contacto cotidiano con la naturaleza, conformando el cuerpo de la cultura material.

En la segunda esfera, se dan las múltiples formas de organización que nos permiten cumplir mejor estas necesidades; el papel que juegan hombres, mujeres, niños y ancianos indica la cantidad de tareas que se tienen que realizar, así como el número de instituciones sociales que han sido creados. La tercera esfera contiene los ingredientes esenciales para nutrir el espiritú y la cultura a través de la religión, el arte, y una cosmovisión particular, creando un cuerpo de símbolos a través de los cuales buscamos nuestros orígenes, le damos significado a nuestros actos en ritos y ceremonias, y embellecemos los objetos que nos rodean.

Las materias primas incorporadas a estos objetos de la cultura material apuntan hacia la relación profunda entre sociedad y naturaleza, en la medida que cada grupo descubre y transforma los recursos vegetales, minerales y animales que les son útiles y que están al alcance de los ecosistemas en su entorno. El valor de la cultura en esta relación se fundamenta en que el conocimiento se acrecenta generación tras generación, en el cual cada grupo (en condiciones normales) se autoimpone vedas y controles para asegurar la sustentabilidad de sus recursos. Menospreciado como conocimiento *empírico* en el mundo científico, en tanto Etnociencia es un cuerpo de conocimiento aplicado, con reglas y lógica propios, que puede ofrecer muchas alternativas hacia el desarrollo sustentable ante la amenaza de desastres ecológicos.

Tambien se relacionan el desarrollo de la tecnología y la industria, pues este es el ámbito donde cada grupo logra realizar su potencial productivo, acorde con el grado de desarrollo tecnólogico y la capacidad organizativa. Entre grupos nómadas de cazadores y recolectores, por ejemplo, cada familia o unidad social tiene que hacer las canastas, cuerdas, lanzas y zaleas de animales que requiere. Por otro lado, es entre los grupos sedentarios, donde ocurre la especialización, y de hecho constituye como tal el origen de la industria, del trueque y del intercambio.

La relación entre tecnología y diseño es uno de los aspectos de las artes populares que menos atención ha recibido. Si miramos a la relación entre forma y función mas de cerca, los cántaros de agua nos proporcionan un excelente ejemplo (Foto 1). Por todo el mundo, uno encuentra que durante miles de años, los mismos principios de física han sido aplicados a los cántaros, resultando en cuatro elementos de diseño. En el problema a resolver, un líquido debe ser procurado a una distancia y transportado por bestia o el hombre mismo; un liquído en marcha se desplaza al doble del movimiento que está sujeto. Por lo que, ¿cuales son las soluciones adoptadas? Una base plana y pequeña, una gran "panza" redondeada, una "boca" estrecha, y dos o tres asas a los lados que facilitan el acarreo y almacenamiento. Ahora bien, resueltos los aspectos técnicos, se dan cientos de variaciones solo para esta forma, por lo que uno llega a la conclusión que la cultura y la identidad se expresan a través del diseño y la decoración de los objetos utilitarios.

El arte y la estética son los elementos a los que uno vincula mas la dimensión cultural de las Artes Populares Mexicanas, pero tal y como las estamos presentando, no son los únicos. Frecuentemente estos aspectos artísticos son una magistral mezcla de cultura, medio ambiente y tecnología. El ingrediente adicional, y que de hecho, provoca la gran diferencia en el impacto visual es la cosmovisión, un elemento altamente abstracto y simbólico del pensamiento mítico, que explica como cada grupo ordena y define los confines del universo—la tierra, el firmamento y el inframundo. En esta esfera, formas y diseños asemejan unidades semánticas cargadas de siginificados: una flecha votiva es un símbolo de comunicación entre seres y deidades; puede diferir de una flecha normal para cazar tan solo por el tipo de plumas, por los dibujos abstractos que tiene pintados, o por el tamaño; donde definitivamente se distingue es en su función, que es enteramente simbólica. Y aunque el papel del simbolismo se visualiza cabalmente en los artefactos ceremoniales y rituales (Foto 58), no excluye enseres utilitarios y su decoración. Al contrario, los códigos estéticos son la suma de unidades básicas de diseño—abstracto o no—que se combinan y recombinan de tal manera que evoluciona un estilo cultural distintivo y siempre identificable (Foto 4).

La extraordinaria diversidad biolólogica de México siempre ha ido de la mano de su diversidad cultural. Mucho antes de la Invasión Española, por lo menos 100 grupos étnicos habitaban las regiones de nuestro pais, cada uno con su propio idioma, filosofía y cultura. Y 500 años mas tarde, 56 grupos todavía ejercen su derecho de practicar su cultura, a pesar de los siglos de opresión y pobreza. Numéricamente continúan siendo los productores mas importantes de Artes Populares y Etnicas.

Las relaciones económicas tambien se dan de manera múltiple en las artes populares. Esta es una esfera donde tiempos de producción, el valor del trabajo, los precios, los mercados y la comercialización entran en juego. En una *economia natural*, todos los objetos de la cultura material producidos dentro de la unidad doméstica y la comunidad circulan internamente, y aún cuando su valor de uso no tiene efectos monetarios, las categorias económicas de costo, tiempo invertido y trabajo están implícitas. Esa cultura no está cuantificando, no importa si una prenda ceremonial llevó un año para tejerse, y se usaron las materias primas mas finas en su realización, porque su finalidad no es la venta (Foto 20).

En contraste, en una *economía mercantil* los bienes se convierten en mercancías que serán cambiadas en un mercado, midiéndose unas y otras con base en el trabajo que tienen incorporado (Foto 56). La fijación de precios, las leyes de la oferta y la demanda, y el intercambio o regateo, se convierten en herramientas esenciales que aprende a manejar el productor. En el *capitalismo*, se incorporan nuevos elementos, ya que la organización de talleres y manufacturas transforman a todo el sistema productivo. A través de la introducción de la privatización de los medios de producción y la contratación de trabajadores, la división del trabajo que surge hace que el dueño le agregue valor a su inversión.

Históricamente en México, (particularmente en las últimas décadas), grupos étnicos cuya cultura material era exclusivamente parte de la economía *natural*, han sido impelidos hacia la economía *mercantil* sin la experiencia y herramientas conceptuales que requieren para no ser explotados. Aún mas reciente, grupos en ambas categorías de autoconsumo y mercantil han encontrado que dada *su* precaria situación de ingresos, un tercer grupo, no relacionado se apodera de los medios y subcontrata la producción a través de la maquila y el trabajo a domicilio, dándole a los artesanos las materias primas, pagándole una miseria por su trabajo.

Otro aspecto que ha surgido es la división detro del artesanado en una pirámide socio-económica bastante definida: cinco porciento están en la cúspide y generalmente son los grandes innovadores (quienes ahora establecen talleres de producción y/o tiendas, aparte de su trabajo artístico por encargo), o artesanos hábiles que ocupan en la venta al mayoreo de artesanias, comprando barato a los artesanos mas pobres; treintaicinco porciento están elaborando copias mas baratas del trabajo de los innovadores, y posiblemente combinándolo con la producción de artesanias mas tradicionales. (Las agencias gubernamentales, los comerciantes y los coleccionistas trabajan mayoritariamente con estos dos grupos.) Y el sesenta porciento restante está apenas sobreviviendo con la producción de los enseres utilitarios mas baratos, o peor todavía, vendiendo su trabajo artístico a los talleres mas exitosos. *Estos artesanos son, por lógica, el sector mas vulnerable*.

Esto nos lleva, por tanto a nuestro último aspecto, aquel donde tenemos que considerar que la cultura es, y siempre ha sido, dinámica. Por lo tanto, es deseable e imperativo ver los *procesos de cambio* sin importar la época. De nuevo, uno tiene que aproximarse desde una óptica multi-disciplinaria, incorporando lo cultural, lo cosmogónico, el medio-ambiente, lo tecnológico, lo artístico y lo económico. Si uno ve lo sucedido en las últimas décadas, tambien tiene que agregar nuevas estrategias de mercado, y el papel de las instituciones gubernamentales, de los organismos públicos y privados, y de los individuos. El cambio puede ser estimulante, y abre todo un mundo de oportunidades para la innovación. Pero el cambio tambien puede ser violento si suceden la sustitución total, la pérdida y la destrucción.

En el mundo de las artes populares, uno de los aspectos mas importantes en este rubro es ¿quien, de hecho, controla la situación? ¿Es que las decisiones vitales artísticas y estéticas están aún en manos del artesano/artista popular, o es que los agentes gubernamentales, las instancias privadas y los individuos le han entregado un patrón que deberán repetir exacta y continuamente?

Por fortuna, el Arte Popular Mexicano es provocativo, no es un campo de trabajo objetivo y frio, está cargado de subjetividad premeditada. Tiene la rara cualidad de volver al observador mas soberbio en el alma mas humilde, y lo que produce el milagro es el contracto con los protagonistas...los artesanos. Creo que todos los que participamos en este sector nos hemos preguntado mil veces, "¿Como es que en un ambiente de trabajo tan austero, con materiales y herramientas tan simples, pueden surgir objetos tan complejos técnicamente, tan armosiosos en diseño y forma, tan sutilmente diferentes el uno del otro aún *dentro del mismo pueblo?*" Y pueden ser radicalmente diferentes de una cultura vecina a otra!

Aún cuando las definiciones en este campo son consideradas riesgosas, en mi obra *Como acercarse a la artesania* publicada en 1988 propongo "que lo que más distingue al artesano del obrero es que el artesano aún conserva una relación vertical e integral con todas y cada una de las fases de producción, desde la obtención de las materias primas hasta la decisión estética final. Este hecho, por insignificante que parezca, hace a nuestro juicio que las dimensiones creativa y artística en la artesania nazcan de la relación intima y simbiótica entre la disciplina y el oficio, entre lo terrenal y lo mítico, es decir, entre la materia y el espiritú."

Los que hemos promovido estas artes tambien estamos concientes de lo injusto que ha sido la historia contemporánea con la artesania.

Creo que muchos nos hemos sentido impotentes mas de una vez ante la magnitud de necesidades de los artesanos aparejada a la magnitud de la pobreza generalizada. La mayor parte de los artesanos dependen de intermediarios y agiotistas que juegan localmente el papel del "mal necesario".

¿Cuantas veces no hemos visto o hemos revivido en el arte popular el viejo cuento de los Conquistadores que trocaron oro por cuentas de vidrio, donde hoy la creatividad y el trabajo se cambian por unas cuantas monedas o unos vasos de aguardiente? ¿Es que la maldición moderna del arte popular será siempre el sacrificio del valor del trabajo frente al precio "competitivo" de venta? ¿Cuando dejará de ser relegado y menospreciado por la historia del arte este supuesto *arte menor*? Por ello, cada camino que uno escoge transitar para apoyar y difundir las artes populares tiene su grado de validez, cada grano de sal aporta a soluciones globales.

Los (Re)Descubrimientos

Curiosamente, nosotros como Estadounidenses y Mexicanos hemos confluído en un mismo espacio a partir de dos raíces e historias diferentes de redescubrimientos. Hasta el advenimiento de la Revolución Industrial, las artesanías eran la única forma de industria que existía. Cuando las máquinas las desplazaron empezaron a aparecer nuevos términos para distinguirlas, tales como *industrias manuales, artes decorativas o artes aplicadas*. Se pronosticó su inevitable muerte y desaparición a manos de la "malvada mecanización", y para contrarrestrarla en Inglaterra surgiría un Movimiento de Artes y Oficios (Arts and Crafts Movement), que enaltecía lo distintivo con el sello de lo Hecho a Mano. Por razones muy diferentes, a principios del Siglo XX, nacientes estados nacionales como México, con una importante población campesina y popular, buscaban símbolos que ayudaran a que se identificaran y unificaran grupos separados social y económicamente durante siglos.

El término Arte Popular se forjó en México a través del enaltecimiento al mestizo—aquel que era el descendiente de la unión entre Cortés y su amante india, La Malinche—en oposición al criollo—el hijo nacido en México de padres españoles. Del mestizo se aduciría que tenia "cualidades intrínsecas, un alma sensible, y el espiritú creador de un pueblo anónimo qaue embellece los objetos útiles por necesidad." Estas artes populares vivieron un efímero momento de gloria junto al Muralismo; artistas famosos como Diego Rivera, Frida Kahlo, el Dr. Atl (Gerardo Murillo), Roberto Montenegro y Miguel Covarrubias lo coleccionaron, lo pintaron, lo promovieron. Y contagiaron a norteamericanos y europeos como William Spratling, Donald y Dorothy Cordry, y René d'Harnoncourt, quienes recorrieron las comunidades mas alejadas a pie, caballo y mula para documentar y formar colecciones privadas o de Museos, ante la amenaza de desaparición que se cernía sobre las artes populares.

Hoy, en los albores del Siglo XXI, sabemos que los pronósticos no se cumplicron, tanto en el mundo industrial como entre las sociedades en camino a la supuesta "modernidad". Pero, y es un gran *pero*, ¿es que todas han sobrevivido? ¿Es que han sobrevivido de la misma manera? Para contestar es necesario ver la situación caso por caso, porque hay artesanías que desaparecieron por completo, como los increíbles enredos (especie de falda) teñidos con cochinilla de grana del Valle de Oaxaca; tambien hay comunidades que han abandonado completamente su actividad artesanal, porque otras fuentes de ingreso y cambios en las pautas de consumo las enterraron. Por otra parte hay comunidades vecinas tales como Teotitlán del Valle y Santa Ana del Valle, donde la actividad textil no solo florece, sino que incorpora a un mayor número de familias que hace cuarenta años. Al mismo tiempo, en mercados nuevos y viejos todavía encuentra uno secciones especializadas en barro utilitario, canastos, petates (o esteras), y metates y molcajetes de piedra que tienen una historia cultural de cientos y hasta miles de años (Foto 3).

Estas son algunas de las preguntas básicas que me he planteado durante los últimos veinte años, y que me han guiado en mis viajes, en mis estudios, en mi trabajo. Por eso cuando a finales de 1991 visité a Annie ONeill en su hogar en New Paltz, en el Estado de Nueva York mi objetivo era definir el enfoque de la exposición *Tradiciones Vivas: Artes Populares de México*, que se integraría mayoritariamente con piezas de su colección. Encontré que compartíamos una época y una visión similar: ubicar que el cambio y las continuidad en las artes populares contemporáneas de México podian abarcar desde *alteraciones imperceptibles*, hasta *transformaciones profundas*. Nuestro deseo conjunto era transmitirle al espectador el mensaje que la vorágine de cambios no están poniendo en riesgo a las tradiciones, sino que la iconografia resultante ha enriquecido la percepción visual de su cultura.

El mejor modo de explicar el cambio sería ahondar en las raices, retroceder sobre las huellas de una comunidad dada y de un artista popular en particular, y tratar de reconstruir los eslabones entre ellos. ¿Como era usado un objeto utilitario en el marco de la cultura que lo requeria? ¿Como respondió el artesano a esta necesidad? ¿Cuales eran las variaciones y evolución en los estilos y su posible origen? ¿En que contribuían para reconstruir el rompecabezas? La colección de Annie ONeill ofrecía estupendos ejemplos de la cultura material inmemorial que podia colocarse en la exposición en dos categorías básicas.

> 1. Fueron mostradas piezas cuya función era utilitaria dentro del hogar y la cocina o usadas como prendas. Esta sección amplia, que entitulamos *Hogar y Fogón*, simboliza el lugar de la mujer, históricamente su espacio de expresión creativa (Foto 10).

> 2. Obras que han sido creadas con fines ceremoniales y religiosas fueron agrupadas en la sección *Arte Popular Ceremonial: Forma y Simbolo*. Incluyó ex-votos, retablos, ángeles, incensarios, candelabros y porta-velas, máscaras, indumentaria ceremonial, figuras usadas para el Dia de Muertos, objetos para altares familiares (Foto 13), y varias ofrendas votivas indigenas. Objetos adicionales prestados para esta sección incluyeron máscaras de la colección del Sr. Eugene Walter y Sra. (Foto 42), y trajes completos de danzas, amablemente prestados por Pilar Gomez (Foto 41).

Las mejor forma de ilustrar el cambio sería mostrando su evolución, con el mayor número posible de ejemplos de estilos y transiciones. En este rubro, la colección de Annie O'Neill tenta ejemplos que caían en dos categorias; una donde el cambio tuvo una base mas bien colectiva y amplia (los pintores de papel de Amate de Guerrero (Foto 39), los indios Huicholes (Foto 54) los alfareros de Ocumicho, los artesanos del maque de Olinalá y Temalacazingo (Foto 14); y la otra, donde individuos innovadores claramente identificados habían creado una mini-revolución en su medio. Se incluyó a Herón Martínez, Teodora Blanco, Josefina Aguilar, Manuel Jiménez, Candelario Medrano, Aurelio Flores, Pedro Linares, Saulo Moreno e Isaac Vasquez.

De esta manera, la amplia sección *Artes Populares en Transición: Artes Nuevas, Tradiciones Viejas*, resaltaría un fenómeno que venía dándose en varios lugares de México desde los años '20 y que había intensificado en el período de la pos-guerra en los años '50. En el mundo artesanal contemporáneo interactúan tres elementos que forman una parábola: bienes culturales se convierten en mercancias, que salen, a su vez, de su ámbito local y regional, para iniciar nuevo camino hacia los hogares de habitantes cosmopolitas del mundo industrializado. En este proceso el artesano se enfrenta a una realidad en la que debe innovar y adaptarse continuamente a las necesidades y gustos del nuevo consumidor, sin perder sus raíces y fundamento cultural. De este modo la cultura, la economía y la innovación forman una malla indisoluble.

Una Era de Transformaciones
Siempre se ha insistido que como actividad, las artesanías generan ingresos que complementan a la agricultura. Uno de los cambios que he notado, es la inversa; *la producción agrícola es la que se ha convertido en la actividad que complementa el ingreso por artesanías de numerosas comunidades artesanales*. Se han reducido las tierra de cultivo disponibles, y las artesanías han llegado a ser mas lucrativas. Sin embargo el vínculo con la tierra y los astros no se pierde, no importa si es minúscula la parcela, y pues sigue sembrando su maíz, el fundamento de la cultura. Junto con esto, tambien ha sido posible observar que se conserva el vínculo religioso a través de la participación de los artesanos en el ciclo anual de fiestas del pueblo; quieren seguir viviendo en su comunidad. Con estos factores, tenemos cierta seguridad que la base de la cultura se mantendrá, aunque cambien las formas exteriores.

La siguiente interrogante es ¿Por que cambian las manifestaciones artesanales? A través de la intervención del consumidor y del cambio del perfil del consumidor, que es quien compra, empiezan los cambios. Cada día son mas los objetos utilitarios del campo que están siendo desplazados por objetos manufacturados industrialmente, porque pueden ofrecerse a menor costo que los artesanales. En ese momento los artesanos tienen que decidir si abandonan la actividad o si se lanzan a la búsqueda de nuevos mercados y alternativas para sus artesanías. Históricamente, el artesano que hace un cántaro, una jarra o un jarrito para vender en el mercado tambien lo ha usado. Esto ha permitido la permanente depuración y purificación del diseño. Ahora le solicitan cafeteras y vajillas que dificilmente usará, por lo que no pasarán por el continuo proceso de perfeccionamiento, requiriendo ayuda técnica externa para resolver problemas en el diseño. Para sobrevivir, los artesanos acaban por adaptar sus objetos a las necesidades del hombre moderno, urbano. Como no es un proceso mecánico e automático, resulta fascinante seguir la secuencia y evolución que ha seguido un artesano en particular o un pueblo entero para llegar a soluciones innovadoras.

En alguna ocasión que releí el libro pionero del Dr. Atl *Las Artes Populares de México* (publicado en 1921), afirma categóricamente que "las industrias indígenas no pueden ni transformarse, ni mejorarse: son lo que son". Y en otra parte de ese mismo capítulo sobre "Las Tendencias de Transformación" reseña una experiencia sucedida en Tonalá, Jalisco en 1915, cuando una persona ajena a la comunidad mandó hacer unos jarros de formas distintas a las tradicionales, solicitando se incorporaran unas grecas aztecas y toltecas. En opinión del autor, el resultado fué catastrófico ya que la loza había perdido su carácter. Ahora bien, el asunto no quedó allí, y nos dice:

> "El instinto artístico de los decoradores de Tonalá fue eliminando poco a poco la imposición del *grequismo* y tomando de los elementos arqueológicos aztecas, toltecas o mayas aquellos que más cuadraban a su propio sentimiento, los aplicaron con sobriedad a las antiguas y a las nuevas formas de vasijas de barro cocido."

Esto reafirmó algo que he observado: para que una innovación logre ser armoniosa, existe una etapa de transición en tanto el artesano se familiariza con las nuevas formas, concepciones y dibujos, en tanto depura lo que para él es superfluo, y le imprime un sello propio, es decir, se apropia del nuevo medio. Es importante seguir documentando estos procesos de cambio que han sucedido en las artesanías desde los años '50, así como tratar de establecer las influencias que recibieron, y establecer las secuencias estilísticas. Una de las grandes interrogantes en este ámbito es si la creatividad y la estética entran en contradicción con las demandas del mercado y las sugerencias temáticas que son hechas por los nuevos consumidores. Igualmente existe la duda si la exaltación de los talentos individuales va en detrimento de la fuente colectiva de inspiración.

¿Cómo se expresan estos cambios?

Lo que caracteriza a la historia de estas artes populares durante siglos, quizás milenios es su *finalidad*: fueron creados como objetos utilitarios para el hogar o tenían un uso litúrgico, ceremonial y ritual. No se encuentra el sentido de lo meramente *decorativo*. Y la gran transformación durante este siglo, ha sido el surgimiento de un arte popular figurativo, casi escultural en su forma, barroco en su estilo, hecho para ser visto y no nececesariamente utilizado (Foto 25). Es más, detrás de cada innovación y de cada innovador existe un objeto o referente cultural como antecedente: detrás de las tablas Huicholas de estambre, existe la *nearica* o la *xicuri*, o jicara votiva (Foto 55); los cántaros pintados fueron la base para los amates pintados (Foto 36); los incensarios y sahumerios han sido convertidos en muñecas y Arboles de la Vida (Foto 27); los silbatos, usados frecuentemente por curanderos (no como juguetes como se nos ha sido informado), se han convertido en lujuriosos diablos; y motivado por la prohibición de la quema de los gigantescos Judas de cartón durante la Semana Santa, en un periodo de diez años se redujeron en tamaño, les salieron cuernos y alas, y nacieron los *alebrijes* (Foto 29).

Nos llena de optimismo la creatividad y genialidad que muestran los artistas populares, pero se vislumbran algunos problemas en su futuro. El éxito comercial de las artes populares y artesanías va aparejada de la sobre-explotación de materias primas, encaminándolos a un desastre ecológico inminente. La falta de programas de protección ambiental y de reforestación para varias especies de árboles que los artesanos requieren (el amate, linaloé, copal, palo fierro), los bejucos, carrizos, palmas y agaves, demandan atención prioritaria. Los artesanos mismos tienen que enfrentar ahora el conocimiento mas avanzado sobre los riesgos de salud. Alfareros que aplican los vidriados de plomo se encuentran con regulaciones y normas cada día mas estrictas para su uso. El elevado costo de transferencia tecnológica está mas allá del alcance de la mayoría; a esto debemos agregar que disminuye la disponibilidad de leña para sus hornos. Hoy dia, la cazuela para el mole y la olla para los frijoles, dos de los objetos mas tradicionales de la cultura culinaria están en peligro de desaparición.

Como coleccionistas, promotores, comerciantes, funcionarios e investigadores hemos interactuado con los artesanos, sugiriéndoles nuevos temas, motivando e incentivando a los mejores y mas creativos, encargándoles obra como *Mecenas de las Artes*, montando exposiciones, organizando concursos que premian la excelencia técnica, la innovación y/o la tradicionalidad. Ante ellos, tenemos una responsabilidad de destacar sus logros, de festejarlos y de apoyarlos. Logramos una gran victoria en 1984 cuando se creó la rama de Artes y Tradiciones Populares como parte del Premio Nacional de Ciencias y Artes de México. Este galardón constituye el reconocimiento mas alto que otorga la nación, y en este casa es la única categoría en la que pueden ser propuestas comunidades, grupos o individuos, acorde con la base colectiva de la creatividad popular. Esta es nuestra contribución. Por fortuna, siempre ha sido, es y será el artesano el que tiene la última palabra. Con su obra hablan por ellos y por mi país.

Marta Turok
Curadora Invitada

Nota de la Curadora: No me queda la menor duda que esta exposición no se hubiera realizado sin el espiritú indomable de Marijo Dougherty. No aceptaba ni una negativa, y en parte se debió a la respuesta entusiasta y entrega total que el H. Patrick Swygert, Presidente de la Universidad de Albany, ha dado a este proyecto. Mil gracias al museógrafo, Zheng Hu, por abrirse al Barroquismo Mexicano cuando entraba en contradicción con la Simplicidad Oriental, a Joanne Lue por su sonrisa vivaz y a Gary Gossen del Departamento de Antropología de la Universidad de Albany, por recomendarme como curadora invitada. Mi mayor y mas sincedro reconocimiento al Consul General Manuel Alonso y a Mireya Terán del Instituto Cultural Mexicano de Nueva York por su apoyo constante, y al Fideicomiso para la Cultura México-Estados Unidos que ha hecho de este catálogo una realidad.

Plate 5, Doña Teodora Blanco (Atzompa, Oaxaca), Grouping of single-fired earthenware figures, 6 x 8 x 4 inches (approx. each figure)

The Artisans and Markets of Mexico: A Collector's View

That magical time in my life—fourteen years of trips to Mexico to collect all things Mexican—began twenty-six years ago. Intense memories and dramatic images are still lingering and inspiring—the high lonely desert of Hidalgo strewn with *maguey*, the facade of Tonanzintla giving way to the wondrous gilded carving within, the ornate folk baroque chapels of the Sierra de Querétaro, the stately *portales* of Cholula, a lone woman wrapped in her ikat *rebozo* beneath a saguaro cactus as tall as a building, the riot of sugar skulls in the old Toluca market, the explosion of fireworks in the Oaxaca *zocalo*, a fiery *mole* in Puebla, trees bending under the weight of tangerines, and pottery—mountains of it—with a diversity of tradition, form and function that has never ceased to capture my imagination. In Mexico, everywhere I turned there was the hand print of woman, of man, of families and communities engaged in creating beautiful objects, churches, towns and landscapes. I will never forget the elaborate yet ephemeral home altars for the *Day of the Dead*, the cactus fences of Zapotec villages, the ruins of Palenque and Monte Alban, the monumental sculpture of La Venta, stone courtyards choked by age-old vines with flowers in colors I only dreamed existed. But most of all, imprinted forever on my mind, and still warm in my heart, are the artisans and the markets!

Mexico is the place where popular arts are a consummate and spontaneous expression, a blend of ancient traditions and cultural and religious beliefs. Travelling and collecting in Mexico has been a never ending treasure hunt that took me to remote mountain villages, weekly markets, seasonal celebrations and lavish fiestas. In Mexico there is such a wealth and richness of traditions that to fully appreciate symbols, design motifs, ritual and form could mean a lifetime of exploration—a lifetime of working through layers of history and mythology searching for origins and sorting out influences. At times the intricacies of this complex world were overwhelming and impenetrable.

In approaching popular arts it was important for me to maintain a certain openness and innocence. An openness and enthusiasm to which I stubbornly cling to this day, knowing at the same time academics and anthropologists are still at the periphery battling out the definitions of folk art. What is traditional, authentic, what is derived, what is tourist art? What aesthetic and cultural values have affected pieces made for an Indian's own use or something made for the collector. Over the years I'm sure many of us have anguished at times over these arguments, but then we forget them and return to collecting with zeal. We all imagine that the degeneration of folk art is occurring at this moment in time, while historically each generation laments the passing of things as they knew them. We have to keep in mind that tradition is often utilitarian and throughout Mexican history there were critical junctures that caused change and upheaval. The Spanish Invasion wrought *enormous* changes, introduced new techniques and crafts; the 19th century was a time of stringent artisan guilds, severe regulation, industrialization, foreign intervention and a war of independence; and of course the Revolution of this century and the "discovery" of folk arts by intellectuals and artists. It is crucial to have a perspective that encompasses time and that allows for a rhythm of change and creativity. What seems like a radical departure in style, form and world view today, might in time prove to be only a minor departure and interesting innovation.

My collection is very personal—a reflection of things in which I delight, and the objects and artisans that intrigued me as I collected. It was not premeditated, it did not adhere to guidelines, nor was it dictated by an adherence to concepts. It documents Mexican popular arts from 1966 to 1981. The exhibition *Living Traditions* focuses intensely on those years—on old forms and new directions and innovations, on traditions skewed by interventions, both internal and external. The exhibition highlights the innovators who came of age in those years: Herón Martinez of Acatlán, Puebla, Teodora Blanco of Santa Maria Atzompa, Oaxaca, the Pedro Linares family of Mexico, D.F., the Aguilars of Ocotlán de Morelos, Oaxaca and Manuel Jiménez of Arrazola, Oaxaca. These were artisans with whom I visited often in those years. Three of them are no longer living (Martinez, Blanco and Pedro Linares) (Plate 6).

Collecting popular arts in Mexico is always an adventure. Awakening early to the incessant clang of church bells, you set out on a crowded bus for a weekly market, and from that moment on you are thrust into a vortex of jostling humanity—a throng of Indians and mestizos intent upon buying, selling, and socializing. You enter a cultural arena and witness age-old rituals that are taking place all over Mexico much as they did in pre-Hispanic times. You are intoxicated by exotic smells and vibrant colors. Moving slowly, packed tightly, you wend your way through a maze of flapping fabric stalls, pushing past squawking chickens and squealing pigs, passing herbal cures and medicinal remedies, past the brilliantly stacked fruits and vegetables, distracted by a slice of pineapple sprinkled with chile powder or a gorgeous mango in season, and then suddenly you see it.... It could be a basket, an incense burner, a carved comb or a push toy, or it could be one water jug in the pile of fifty. But it is there for *you*. And it is that moment of discovery that for most collectors is the excitement that kindles the quest. Often you make the vendor's first sale of the day. She crosses herself; you silently cross yourself for your luck in finding that special piece. You know there will never be another! Out of those hundred painted *pulque* jars that look alike to the uninitiated, you find the one that speaks a different language. The painting has an energy and expressiveness that sets it apart, and the form is more beautiful. This might sound like a strange fabrication, but remember that within the village of potters, the artisans can always distinguish each other's work. In the highlands of Chiapas each woman knows the language of the other weavers, each one can tell the quality, the time taken and the symbolic language of the embroidery. We might think of these artisans as anonymous. Hardly! So I say to all prospective collectors to look carefully, don't ever be fooled by a surface similarity, don't glaze over when confronted by a quantity of sarapes or by twenty embroidered blouses. Enter into that world, understanding that each piece is hand-made. Little differences are not minor aberrations, *they are aesthetic decisions and personal choices*.

I discovered Mexico, its artisans, markets, and culture in the mid-1960s after a whirlwind trip that had a profound affect on my life. As a peripheral child of the 60s my personal battle against technology and the machine-made was simmering. It was in Mexico that I saw another way of life: men and women and families making things that they always had made, the things they needed, and that others needed, leading lives enriched by ceremonies and fiestas, lives in tune with agricultural cycles. This was all quite an overwhelming experience for me, one that changed the course of my life.

In 1966 I opened the Mexican Folk Art Annex, a gallery shop hidden away on the third floor of a loft building in midtown Manhattan. It was the beginning of a fourteen-year love affair with Mexico. I look back with some astonishment to think that in the summer of that year I was a floundering college graduate and within three months, with the encouragement and help of devoted parents, I was in business. I was able to blend my craft and art background with social concerns and also have a business selling and exhibiting objects that touched other peoples imaginations and enriched their lives. The only trouble was that it was hidden away, but within two years I moved to a second floor loft closer to Fifth Avenue on 56th Street. My gallery-shop became the focal point for collectors and aficionados.

My store was discovered by Nelson Rockefeller in 1968, then the Governor of New York State. Fortuitously his office was right around the corner. *He* was also a great discovery for *me*—a renowned collector who felt passionate about the same pieces I so loved. As governor of New York from 1959 to 1973, political life absorbed most of his energies, but his feelings for Mexican folk art were always near the surface. One day on his way home from his office, he looked up and saw my store. I still clearly remember his first visit. It was after five o'clock, and the shop was closed. When I looked through the peephole to decide whether or not to let one last person in, I thought I had better let that tired looking man have a look. What a surprise to discover that man was the Governor! An even greater treat was to watch him voraciously assimilate everything on all the shelves and in every corner. After a few minutes he looked like a different person—he had been energized. His old interest was alive again.

Soon after this visit, he had all the old boxes in the basement of Rockefeller Center reopened after twenty-eight years and began planning an exhibition of his Mexican folk art collection for the Museum of Primitive Art. He wanted to update the collection and sent me to Mexico in search of contemporary pieces to fill the gaps.

When the shipment arrived, he carefully checked every inch of the storeroom, often on his knees, searching for pieces he might have missed. The 1969 exhibition was for Rockefeller a personal triumph in his battle to have folk art recognized in major museums, a battle he still waged with the Metropolitan Museum of Art. He would have been deeply saddened that the Metropolitan did not include folk art in their recent extravaganza *Mexico: Thirty Centuries of Splendor*.

Rockefeller continued adding to his collection throughout the 1970s, bringing friends and colleagues by and always encouraging their interest. I was able to be a guiding eye and fill him in on changes and developments. When he retired from politics in 1977 he announced he would prepare a series of five books on his personal collections. The Mexican folk art collection would be one of those books. In late October 1978, in time for the *Dia de los Muertos*, a group of us, including his daughter Ann, went with him to Mexico to set the mood for the project. I planned a strenuous itinerary for our four days in Oaxaca and the surrounding villages. We bought enthusiastically in local markets and visited many of the valley's innovators including Teodora Blanco, Manuel Jiménez, and Doña Rosa.

Rockefeller loved the physical and emotional contact a market place is all about, and his excitement was infectious. When Rockefeller died the following January, I continued to work with his daughter Ann, organizing the collection which she bought from the estate, searching for its final museum home, and completing the book *Folk Treasures of Mexico, The Nelson A. Rockefeller Collection* (Abrams 1990). His collection was eclectic and personal, and reflected the 1930s, his most active period of collecting.

Over the years I was involved in some serious adventures in Mexico. My good friend, the late Carlos Espejel who wrote extensively about ceramics, folk toys, and popular arts, was Director of the *Museo de Artes y Industrias Populares* in the middle 70s. Before that he was at Banfoco, one of the initial government organizations to promote popular arts. In 1973 he helped me organize a show of Pedro Linares' paper *alebriges*, and after that I organized many small exhibits highlighting my favorite artisans. In 1975 I travelled throughout Mexico with Carlos working on his book *Artesania Popular Mexicana*. In those days we travelled by horseback to San Pablito, Puebla in search of embroideries and to observe the production of bark paper. We flew into Jesus Maria, Nayarit to see and document the Cora's Holy Week celebration, and made many trips to my favorite markets in Cuetzalan, Ixmiquilpan, and Huehutla. We drove through the Sierra de Puebla, the Sierra Madre del Sur in Oaxaca, the tropical areas of Vera Cruz, and the semi-tropical mountains of San Luis Potosí. We visited artisans throughout Michoacán, collecting and documenting ceramics. It was a very exciting time in my life. I met artisans from all over Mexico. I shared tortillas and *frijoles* with copper workers from Santa Clara del Cobre, and fruit tamales with lacquer artisans at the opening of the Lacquerware Museum in Chiapa de Corzo.

Carlos was part of so many artisans' families, not only as a mentor, adviser and buyer, but also as a *compadre*. It was a rare experience to be able to see the love that these people felt for him, and the care and respect he had for them. He was able to nurture their spirit of creativity with an energy necessary to perpetuate crafts that were on the brink of death. He understood the delicate balance between old traditions and new market demands and was able to guide artisans along a course that didn't compromise skills and techniques.

I worked on a book about Olinalá lacquerware with Carlos in 1975. A then remote town in the Sierra Madre del Sur of Guererro, Olinalá was accessible only by small plane on clear still days. We would arrive in the middle of a corn field and within an hour great feasts were spread out in each house we visited. At night we ate turkey *mole* while music was played until no one could stay awake any longer. His philosophical outlook profoundly influenced me. Although he lamented the passing of the older artisans and the disappearance of many arts, he never had the negativity of those people who only look backward and are blindly intolerant of innovation. He focused on artisans and tenaciously tried not to be bogged down by the intricacies of the political system and the opposing bureaucratic egos colliding over policy-making at the expense of village craftspeople.

The late 60s and early 70s were an unusual time to be involved with Mexican folk arts. It was a critical time for artisans. The government was fostering programs to ensure the survival of folk art and was encouraging innovation. Many traditional forms were being embellished or modified to be economically viable. In the late 60s people suddenly woke up and realized that very little attention had been paid to these artisans, and if it wasn't, popular arts would be lost forever. At this juncture wars were beginning between the anthropological purists and cultural preservationists. Those rooted in tradition and continuity were bombarded with all these changes and lamented the demise of the folk artist. Their sometimes insular vision, full of romanticism and nostalgia, was being shattered by the reality of the abandonment of age-old forms. Why carry a clay *cántaro* for miles, when you can use plastic? Why weave a basket of palm or spend a year weaving and embroidering a *huipil* when you can buy a contemporary dress in the market? We often forget that new materials and techniques are as seductive to Indians as they are to us.

Looking back over those fourteen years of going back and forth to Mexico, I realize that it was difficult to be a systematic collector while wearing so many hats: shopkeeper, adviser, artist and collector. Many of the most extraordinary pieces I bought are in private collections around this country and in Europe. I never kept any of the fine *cántaros* or other utilitarian pottery, gone are the enormous *trees of life* and superb masks and intricately embroidered *huipils*. Many of these things are no longer made. There was no way I could have hoarded it all, but I still dream about pieces I should have kept. Above all, I regret not keeping a diary and documenting the pieces I did collect. It is something all collectors should do since time makes everything just a little bit fuzzy and swallows up details.

Collecting Mexican popular art is a multi-faceted experience—the pieces I love appeal to me on so many different levels. They open up a whole world. I remember where and from whom I bought them. Then that layer unfolds and I begin to remember the town, the market, or the artisan's workshop. And soon the pieces are suffused with many memories. I look around me at home and have my own three-dimensional scrapbook. If some visitor is disturbed by the wildly painted skeletons or leering devils, my flying dragons, or hundreds of miniatures, if they think that many things seem rough around the edges or too playful for a grown-up, then I secretly feel sorry that they have not immersed themselves in the magical world that is Mexico. These special pieces cannot always be understood through just the eyes...the heart and imagination must be at work too.

Annie O'Neill
September 1992

Author's note: I would like to thank Marijo Dougherty, Associate Director of the University Art Museum, who was able to see that in my sometimes haphazard and eclectic accumulations, there was not only an exhibition waiting to be organized, but there was also an embarrassment of riches. Working with Marijo and the brilliant designer Zheng Hu of the museum staff was an experience no collector should ever miss. Having the support of the University at Albany and the enthusiastic attention and personal concern of University President Swygert made this whole experience not only possible but remarkable as well. Marta Turok imbrued the project with a clarity of vision that brought together all the facets and implications of living traditions in Mexican popular arts.

Artesanos Y Mercados De Mexico: La Vision De Una Coleccionista

Ese tiempo mágico en mi vida—catorce años de viajes a México para coleccionar todo lo mexicano—comenzó hace veintiseis años. Imágenes dramáticas y recuerdos intensos todavía me inundan e inspiran—el desierto de Hidalgo sembrado de magueyes, la fachada de Tonanzintla como preámbulo de las maravillas labradas y doradas de su interior, las capillas populares barrocas de la Sierra de Querétaro, los imponentes portales de Cholula, una mujer envuelta en su rebozo de *ikat* bajo un sahuaro tan alto como un edificio, el goce con las calaveras de azúcar del antiguo mercado de Toluca, la explosión de juegos pirotécnicos en el zócalo de Oaxaca, un feroz mole en Puebla, árboles que se doblan por el peso de las mandarinas, y loza -montañas de loza- con una diversidad de tradiciones, formas y funciones que nunca han dejado de capturar mi imaginación. En México, sin importar donde volteara, estaba la seña de una mujer, de un hombre, de familias y comunidades, avocados a crear bellos objetos, iglesias, pueblos y paisajes. Nunca olvidaré los primorosos y efímeros altares hogareños casa para los Días de Muertos, las bardas de cactus de los pueblos zapotecos, las ruinas de Palenque y Monte Albán, la escultura monumental de La Venta, patios de piedra sofocados por viejas enredaderas con flores cuyos colores solo había imaginado en sueños. Pero ante todo, la huella mas indeleble que queda en mi memoria, y vive aún en mi corazón es la de los artesanos y los mercados.

México es el lugar donde las artes populares son una expresión consumada y espontánea, una mezcla de tradiciones antiguas y creencias culturales y religiosas. Viajar y coleccionar en México ha sido una búsqueda de tesoros sin fin, que me llevó a los pueblos mas aislados entre las montañas, a mercados semanales, a celebraciones estacionales y las fiestas mas pródigas. En México hay tanta abundancia y riqueza de tradiciones, que para apreciar de lleno los símbolos, diseños, rituales y formas significaría dedicar toda una vida a explorarlos—una vida entre capas de historia y mitología buscando los orígenes y separando las influencias. En ocasiones los laberintos de este mundo tan complejo eran abrumadores e inpenetrables.

Al acercarme a las artes populares fue importante para mi mantener una apertura e inocencia; una apertura y entusiasmo que procuro conservar hasta el presente, a sabiendas que los académicos y antropólogos siguen en la periferia debatiendo las definiciones de arte popular. ¿Que es tradicional, auténtico, que es derivación, que es arte para turistas? ¿Cuales son los valores culturales y estéticos que han afectado a las piezas hechas para el uso de un indio o elaboradas especialmente para el coleccionista? A través de los años estoy segura que muchos de nosotros nos hemos angustiado en ocasiones por estos argumentos, pero se nos olvidan y regresamos a coleccionar con singular ahínco. Todos llegamos a imaginarnos que la degeneración del arte popular está ocurriendo en este momento, en tanto que se ha visto que históricamente cada generación se lamenta de las cosas que ellas conocieron y que ahora han cambiado. Debemos recordar que la tradición es frecuentemente utilitaria y que a través de la historia de México se dieron coyunturas críticas que causaron cambios y trastornos. La Conquista Española provocó *tremendos* cambios, introdujo nuevas técnicas y artesanías; el siglo XIX fue una época de estrictos gremios de artesanos, regidos por severas ordenanzas, industrialización, intervención extranjera y una guerra de Independencia; y por supuesto la Revolución de este siglo y el "descubrimiento" de las artes populares por los intelectuales y artistas. Es fundamental tener una perspectiva que engloba el tiempo y que se abre a los ritmos de cambio y creatividad. Lo que parece hoy en día como algo radicalmente diferente en términos de estilo, forma y visión del mundo, podrá mañana ser tan solo una pequeña variante e innovación interesante.

Mi colección es muy personal—refleja las cosas que me deleitan, y los objetos y artesanos que me intrigaron en mi proceso de compras. No fue premeditado, no se adhirió a pautas preestablecidas, ni fué dictada por una linea conceptual. Lo que sí logra es documentar las Artes Populares de 1966 a 1981. La exposición *Tradiciones Vivas* se enfoca intensamente sobre aquellos años—e incluye tanto formas antiguas como nuevas direcciones e innovaciones, al igual que tradiciones sesgadas por injerencias, internas y externas. La exposición acentúa a los innovadores que se proyectaron en esos años: Herón Martínez de Acatlán, Puebla, Teodora Blanco de Santa Maria Atzompa, Oaxaca, la Familia de Pedro Linares de la ciudad de México, las hermanas Aguilar de Ocotlán de Morelos, Oaxaca y Manuel Jiménez de Arrazola, Oaxaca. Estos son los artesanos que frecuenté durante ese período. Tres de ellos ya no viven (Martinez, Blanco y Pedro Linares) (Foto 6).

Coleccionar artes populares en México siempre resulta una aventura. Al despertar temprano a las constantes campanadas de una iglesia, aborda uno el camión apretujado hacia un mercado semanal, y a partir de ese momento se encuentra uno entre una marea humana—una multitud de indígenas y mestizos resueltos a comprar, vender y socializar. Se inmersa uno en una arena cultural y atestigua rituales milenarios que se suceden por todo México, igual como ocurrieron en tiempos Pre-hispánicos. Se intoxica uno por olores exóticos y colores vibrantes. Moviédose despacito, apretujada, sigue uno el camino entre laberintos de puestos con telas que aletean, a empujones pasa uno las gallinas con su quiquiriqueo y los cerdos con sus chillidos, pasa uno las ventas de hierbas medicinales, pasa uno las frutas y legumbres amontonadas y fulgorosas, se distrae uno con una rebanada de piña espolvoreada como polvo de chile piquín o un precioso mango en temporada, y de pronto lo descubre uno…Puede ser un canasto, o un sahumerio, o un peine labrado o un juguete para empujar, o puede ser uno entre cincuenta cántaros. Pero es a **tí** a quien está aguardando. Y ese momento de descubrimiento es para la mayor parte de coleccionistas la emoción que enciende la mecha de la búsqueda. Frecuentemente es la primer venta del día para el vendedor. Ella se persigna; y uno se persigna en silencio por la buena suerte de hallar esa pieza tan especial. Uno sabe que ¡nunca habrá otra igual! Entre los cientos de jarros pintados para pulque, que el neófito los vé igual, es el coleccionista el que elige aquel que se expresa en un lenguaje diferente. Su decoración proyecta una energía y una expresión que la separa de los demás, y la forma es más bella. Podrá sonar como una extraña maquinación, pero recuerde que dentro de un pueblo alfarero, los artesanos pueden distinguir el trabajo de unos y otros. En los altos de Chiapas cada mujer conoce el lenguaje de las demás tejedoras, cada una puede distinguir la calidad, el tiempo y el lenguaje simbólico

Pedro Linares, Installation View, University Art Museum, 1992

de los diseños. Quizás consideremos a estos artesanos como productores anónimos. ¡Nada más alejada de la verdad—! Ese es el consejo que le doy a todos los coleccionistas novatos, que se fijen, que nunca se dejen engañar por una similitud aparente, que no den un mero vistazo ante un cerro de sarapes o una veintena de blusas bordadas. Es necesario compenetrarse en ese mundo, y comprender que cada pieza está hecha a mano. Pequeñas diferencias no son tan solo aberraciones menores, *son ante todo decisiones estéticas y preferencias personales*.

Descubrí México, sus artesanos, mercados y cultura a mediados de los años '60 después de un viaje relámpago que tuvo un profundo efecto sobre mi vida. Como una criatura periférica de los '60 mi batalla personal en contra de la tecnología y lo hecho a máquina estaba hirviendo. Fué en México donde pude ver formas alternativas de vida: hombres, mujeres y familias haciendo cosas que siempre habían hecho, las que ellos necesitaban, las que requerían otros, llevando vidas enriquecidas por los ciclos de ceremonias y fiestas, viviendo en armonía con los ciclos agrícolas. Esta experiencia me abrumó, pero tambien cambió el curso de mi vida.

En 1966 abrí el Mexican Folk Art Annex, una galería-tienda escondida en el tercer piso de un desván en el medio de Manhattan. Sería el comienzo de un amasiato de catorce años con México. Cuando hecho una mirada hacia atrás pienso con asombro que era una vacilante graduada universitaria, y en menos de tres meses, con el estímulo y apoyo de mis devotos padres, ya tenía un negocio. Pude combinar mis conocimientos sobre arte y artesanías con mis inquietudes sociales y tambien tener un negocio que exhibiera y vendiera objetos que tocara la imaginación de otros y enriqueciera sus vidas. El ùnico problema era que estaba escondida la tienda, pero para el segundo año me mudé a un desván en un segundo piso mas cercano a la Quinta Avenida, sobre la calle 56, y pronto mi galería-tienda se convirtió en el centro de reunión de coleccionistas y aficionados.

Mi local fué descubierto por Nelson Rockefeller en 1968, cuando todavía se desempeñaba como Gobernador del Estado de Nueva York. De manera fortuita su oficina estaba a la vuelta. El fué tambien un gran descubrimiento para mí—un coleccionista renombrado que sentía la misma pasión por las piezas que yo tanto amaba. Como gobernador de Nueva York entre 1959-1973, el ambiente político absorbía la mayor parte de sus energías, pero sus sentimientos hacia el Arte Popular Mexicano siempre afloraron. Un día de regreso a casa, volteó hacia arriba y vió mi tienda. Todavía recuerdo su primer visita. Ya pasaban de las cinco de la tarde, y la tienda había cerrado. Cuando me asomé por el atisbadero para decidir si dejaría entrar o no a ese último cliente, pensé que sería mejor dejar pasar a ese hombre tan cansado. ¡Que sorpresa me llevé al descubrir que ese hombre era el mismísimo Gobernador! Mayor agasajo fue verlo asimilar vorazmente todo lo que estaba en los anaqueles y en cada esquina. Después de unos cuantos minutos se transformó

—se había vigorizado. Su añejo interés había revivido.

No mucho tiempo después de su visita, reabrió todas las viejas cajas que tenía en el sótano del Centro Rockefeller desde hacía veintiocho años, y que habrían estado destinados a una exposición de su colección de Arte Popular Mexicano para el Museo de Arte Primitivo. Quería actualizar la colección y me envió a México en busca de piezas contemporáneas que llenaran los huecos.

Cuando llegó el envío, cuidadosamente revisó cada centímetro de la bodega, muchas veces arrodillado, para asegurarse que no se le hubiera escapado una sola pieza. La exposición de 1969 fue un pequeño triunfo para Rockefeller en su lucha por el reconocimiento del Arte Popular en los grandes museos, una batalla que siguió librando con el Museo Metropolitano de Arte. Le hubiera entristecido profundamente que el Metropolitano no haya incluído al arte popular en su reciente *extravaganza México: Treinta Siglos de Esplendor*.

Rockefeller continuó acrecentando su colección durante la década de los '70, invitando a colegas y amigos a que la vieran para propiciar su interés. Mi papel fue de guiarle, de informarle sobre cambios y evoluciones. Cuando se retiró de la política en 1977 anunció que prepararía una serie de cinco libros sobre sus colecciones personales. La colección de Arte Popular Mexicano sería uno de ellos. A finales de octubre de 1978 con motivo de las celebraciones de los Días de Muertos, lo acompañamos a México un grupo de personas incluyendo a su hija Ann, para ambientar el proyecto. El itinerario que les preparé fué intensivo y extensivo, para pasar cuatro días en la ciudad de Oaxaca y pueblos aledaños. Compramos con entusiasmo en los mercados locales y visitamos a muchos de los innovadores incluyendo a Teodora

37

Blanco, Manuel Jiménez y Doña Rosa. Rockefeller se nutría con el contacto físico y la carga emotiva que representaban los mercados, y sus ánimos nos contagiaban. Cuando falleció el siguiente 1o de Enero, continué trabajando con su hija Ann, organizando la colección que ella le compró a la sucesión, buscando el museo donde se legaría, y completando el libro *Folk Treasures of México, The Nelson A. Rockefeller Collection*, editado por Abrams en 1990. Su colección era ecléctica y personal, y reflejaba ante todo el Arte Popular de la década de los 1930.

A través de los años me involucré en algunas aventuras importantes. Mi buen amigo, el recién fallecido Carlos Espejel, que escribió ampliamente sobre alfarería, juguetes populares, y artes populares, dirigía—a mediados de los años '70—, el *Museo Nacional de Artes e Industrias Populares*. Antes de esto había estado en Banfoco, una de las primeras instituciones gubernamentales avocadas a la promoción de las artes populares. En 1973 me auxilió en la organizaciòn de una exposición de los alebrijes de cartón y papel de Pedro Linares, y despúes de eso organicé varias exposiciones pequeñas resaltando a mis artesanos favoritos. En 1975 acompañé a Carlos por todo México mientras hacía su libro *Artesanía Popular Mexicana*. En esos tiempos viajamos todavía a caballo para llegar a San Pablito Pahuatlán, Puebla para buscar tejidos y bordados, y para documentar la producción del papel de amate. Entramos por avioneta a Jesus Maria, Nayarit para presenciar y documentar la Semana Santa Cora, y también hicimos muchos viajes a mis mercados consentidos en Cuetzalan, Ixmiquilpan y Huehuetla. Recorrimos la Sierra de Puebla, la Sierra Madre del Sur en Oaxaca, las áreas tropicales de Veracruz, y las montañas semi-áridas de San Luis Potosí. Visitamos a los artesanos de todo Michoacán, coleccionando y documentando la alfarería. Fueron momentos muy estimulantes en mi vida. Conocí a artesanos de todos los rincones de México. Compartí las tortillas y frijoles con artesanos del cobre de Santa Clara del Cobre y tamales de frutas con artesanos de laca en la inauguración del Museo de la Laca en Chiapa de Corzo.

Carlos formaba parte de la familia de tantos artesanos, no solo como un guía, consejero y comprador, sino también como compadre. Representaba una extraordinaria oportunidad ver el amor que sentían por él, y el cariño y respeto que él les profesaba. Tenía la capacidad de nutrirles su espíritu creativo con la energía que se requería para revitalizar artesanías que estaban a punto de desaparecer. Comprendía el delicado equilibrio entre las viejas tradiciones y las nuevas demandas del mercado, y encauzaba a los artesanos sobre un camino que no comprometía la destreza con las técnicas.

Trabajé con Carlos en la elaboración de un libro sobre Olinalá en 1975. Todavía era una comunidad remota enclavada en la Sierra Madre del Sur de Guerrero, y se llegaba únicamente por avioneta en días claros y apacibles. Aterrizábamos a la mitad de una milpa y al cabo de una hora grandes festejos y banquetes estaban preparados en cada casa que visitábamos. Por la noche comíamos mole de guajolote, escuchando música hasta que nos caíamos del sueño. Su visión filosófica me influenció profundamente. Aún cuando se lamentaba la muerte de los viejos artesanos, y con ello la desaparición de muchas artes, nunca mostró esa negatividad que se asocia a las personas que se encierran en el pasado y son intolerantes de las innovaciones. Se enfocó en el bienestar de los artesanos y tenazmente evitó empantanarse con las jugaretas de las personas dentro de la burocracia y de los vericuetos del sistema político, para evitar entrar en conflicto sobre políticas de estado a expensas de los artesanos.

El final de los años '60 y el inicio de los años '70 fueron una época especial para estar involucrada en las artes populares mexicanas. Para los artesanos fue una época crítica. El gobierno estaba fomentando programas para asegurar la supervivencia del arte popular y estaba auspiciando la innovación.

Muchas de las formas tradicionales se estaban ornamentando o modificando para hacerlas viables económicamente. A finales de los '60 muchas personas de dieron cuenta que los artesanos estaban recibiendo muy poca atención, y si no se corregía, las artes populares se perderían para siempre. Fué en esta coyuntura que se desataron las guerras entre los antropólogos puristas y los conservacionistas culturales. Los que estaban enraizados en la tradición y la continuidad se sentían abrumados por los cambios, y lamentaban la desaparición del artesano. Su visión algo estrecha, llena de romanticismo y nostalgia, se estaba haciendo añicos ante la realidad del abandono de formas antiguas. ¿Para qué cargar un cántaro kilómetros, cuando se puede usar plástico? ¿Por qué tejer un canasto de palma o tardar un año tejiendo y brocando un huipil, si en el mercado se podía comprar un vestido moderno? Frecuentemente nos olvidamos que los nuevos materiales y técnicas le son tan seductivos a los indígenas, como nos resultan a nosotros.

Al voltear la mirada a esos catorce años de ir y venir a México, me doy cuenta de lo difícil que era ser una coleccionista sistemática, mientras me ponía tantas *camisetas*: tendera, consejera, artista y coleccionista. Muchas de las piezas mas extraordinarias que adquirí forman parte de colecciones privadas de Estados Unidos y Europa. Nunca me quedé con los cántaros mas finos, o con la alfarería utilitaria; ya salieron de mis manos los enormes *árboles de la vida* y las magníficas máscaras y huipiles profusamente decorados. Muchas de estas cosas ya no se producen. No hay modo que yo hubiera podido atesorarlas, pero todavía sueño con algunas piezas que debería haber conservado. De lo que sí me arrepiento es no haber guardado un diario y haber sido mas cuidadosa en documentar las piezas que sí coleccioné. Es algo que todo coleccionista debe hacer, porque el tiempo borra y se traga los detalles.

Coleccionar Arte Popular Mexicano es una experiencia polifacética, las piezas que mas quiero me llevan a reflexionar en tantos niveles, además de abrirme todo un mundo. Recuerdo donde y a quien se los compré. Luego paso al segundo nivel y comienzo a recordar el pueblo, el mercado, o el taller del artesano. Y pronto las piezas se saturan de memorias. Aquí en la intimidad de mi casa, al mirar a mi alrededor es como si tuviera un álbum de recuerdos tri-dimensional. Si algùn visitante se escandaliza ante las calacas caprichosamente pintadas, o los diablos de mirada lasciva, o mis dragones voladores, o cientos de miniaturas; si piensan que muchas piezas parecen toscas en el acabado, o demasiado juguetonas para un adulto, secretamente me produce lástima que no se hayan inmerso en ese mundo mágico que es México. Estas piezas especiales no pueden comprenderse solo a través de los ojos...el corazón y la imaginación tambien entran en juego.

Annie O'Neill

Nota de la autora: Quisiera agradecer a Marijo Dougherty, Directora Adjunta del Museo de Arte Universitario, quien percibió que entre tanta acumulación fortuita y ecléctica, no solo había una exposición que aguardaba ser organizada, sino que tambien había un cúmulo de riquezas casi vergonzosas. Trabajar con Marijo y el brillante diseñador Xheng Hu del personal del Museo fué una experiencia que ningùn coleccionista debe perderse. Haber contado con el apoyo de la Universidad de Albany y la personal y entusiasta respuesta del Rector de la Universidad el señor Swygert quienes han hecho que toda esta experiencia haja sido no solo posible, sino memorable. Marta Turok imbuyó al proyecto gran claridad de visión que hizo posible que se conjuntaran todas las facetas e implicaciones de las tradiciones vivas en las Artes Populares Mexicanas.

Plate 7
Green Water Jug (Chililico, Hildago)
8 x 8 inches.

Introduction

*L*iving Traditions: Mexican Popular Arts is a visual essay that considers change and continuity among artisans, their crafts, and the purposes for which these objects are created. These popular art forms provide the opportunity to document, through visual evidence, the processes of *culture in motion*. In particular, we are able to observe the dynamic results of what happens to material culture and popular art when cultures come into contact with one another.

We are able to appreciate the continuity between the graceful lines of a clay water jug that sits in the corner of a contemporary Mexican thatched-roof hut, and the very similar form of its thousand-year-old ancestral vessel that today sits in a museum. By observing the similarity between an intricately carved mask, as depicted in the representation of a ritual dance in a pre-Hispanic codex, and the modern derivative form that is currently used in devotional rituals in honor of the Virgin of Guadalupe, it is possible to delve into the probable functional meaning of both objects, ancient and modern. At the same time, we can marvel at the works of innovators, such as the late Pedro Linares, whose surrealistic papier-mâché figures *alebriges* he attributed to designs inspired by hallucinations that came to him during a prolonged illness some 40 years ago.

We are able to sense intuitively that, despite the evident differences in the origins of these objects, and in the transformation of their form and function from ancient times to the present, they all have something in common; *the driving cultural force has not changed*. Hence, the concept of living traditions in Mexican Popular Art is not a contradiction. New crafts and old folk arts forms are clearly related, for the old forms never died. They continue to be recreated and transformed in each new generation.

Tradiciones Vivas: Artes Populares Mexicanas es un ensayo visual sobre el cambio y la continuidad entre artesanos, las artesanías que producen y el consumidor final. Ellas nos proveen una singular oportunidad para documentar la dinámica cultura, dado que aportan elementos tangibles de la permanente influencia que ejercen entre si las culturas en contacto.

Hoy en día podemos recrear nuestra vista tanto con las lineas mas fluidas y sencillas de un cántaro de agua que cuelga de la esquina de un jacal con techo de palma, y cuyo pariente milenario occupa una vitrina en un museo; podemos escudriñar el origen y significado de una máscara profusamente tallada que podemos identificar en una danza ritual de algún códice Prehispánico, y que ahora se usa como ofrenda a la Virgen de Guadalupe; y tambien podemos maravillarnos ante los grandes artistas populares innovadores, como el recién fallecido Pedro Linares, creador de las figuras surrealistas de papel y cartón que bautizó como alebrijes, y que atribuyó a las alucinaciones que tuvo en el transcurso de una larga enfermedad, hará unos 40 años.

Aún cuando sea solo de manera intuitiva, logramos percibir que dentro de las grandes diferencias en origen, y de las transformaciones que han tenido en su forma y su función, todas nos transmiten un mensaje similar: que lo que no ha cambiado es la fuerza cultural que los impulsa, y es por esto que la tradición viva en las Artes Populares Mexicanas no entra en contradicción con nuevas expresiones artesanales y viejas formas artísticas.

Home and Hearth:
Life Cycles

For thousands of years utilitarian objects were created in response to the specific needs our ancestors had for food, shelter and clothing. The form of an object was greatly determined by the function it was to serve: the simple flowing lines of a water jug's big belly and closed neck allowed for water to be transported without spilling; simple tools did not hinder the development of complex techniques, and within this delicate balance each culture applied unique design elements that enhanced the aesthetic qualities of the humblest materials nature provided—clay and fiber.

Home and Hearth have been traditionally the woman's realm—the perfect setting for the development of basket weaving, pottery, and textiles. In addition to the kitchen it has been the place where Mexican women expressed their creativity and applied their knowledge. Mexican cuisine is renowned, as are the textile arts of past and present and as potter, basket maker and weaver, women played an historical role in the development of the tools and techniques used to manufacture utilitarian wares. With the Spanish Invasion and the influx of new materials and techniques men were incorporated into the more economically viable workshops.

Hogar y Fogon
Durante miles de años se crearon objetos utilitarios en respuesta a las necesidades que tenían nuestros ancestros para comida, abrigo y cobijo. La forma de un objeto estaba determinada en gran parte por la función que iba a servir: así, las lineas sencillas de un cántaro de agua con su gran panza y boca cerrada permitía que se transportara el agua sin que se tirara; las herramientas mas sencillas no impidieron que se desarrollaran las técnicas mas complejas, y dentro de este delicado equilibrio cada cultura aplicó sus propios elementos de diseño, resaltando las cualidades estéticas de los materiales mas humildes que nos provee la naturaleza: el barro y las fibras.

El Fogón, y el Hogar an sido tradicionalmente el reino de las mujeres-el marco perfecto para el desarrollo de la cestería, de la alfareria, y de los textiles. Además, la cocina ha sido el lugar donde las mujeres Mexicanas expresan su creatividad y aplican sus conocimientos. Tan conocida es la Cocina Mexicana, como las Artes Textiles del pasado y el presente; y en su papel de alfarera, tejedora de cestas y de ropa, las mujeres jugaron un papel histórico en el desarrollo de las herramientas y técnicas aplicadas para elaborar objetos utilitarios. Con la Invasion Española, y la llegada de nuevos materiales y técnicas, los hombres se incorporaron a los talleres de producción.

Plate 8
Jacinto Rojas, *Kitchen View with Bedroom*, IX-29-80, oil on canvas, 48 x 32 inches.

Paintings Of Jacinto Rojas

Jacinto Rojas is one of Mexico's finest painters of backdrop murals, the large canvases used by itinerant photographers who travel throughout Mexico to religious festivals and large regional markets. These photographers set up their oversized murals, often painted with religious themes or rural landscapes, and have an assortment of props (a sombrero, sarape, rebozo or large stationery horse) with which to dress or pose their subjects—young and old, families, couples, Indians or *mestizos*. The photograph, developed on the spot and put into a little paper frame, becomes the cherished memory of attendance at a revered Cathedral, a religious pilgrimage, an annual market or important religious *fiesta*.

    I first met Jacinto Rojas at La Villa near the Basilica de Guadalupe, one of Mexico's important religious sites. His large murals were set up there, and on days when he isn't painting he will be there photographing. I loved his style of painting and was immediately struck by his sense of perspective, his wonderful people, naive spacial relationships and unusual way of painting shadows. I certainly couldn't bring home one of his murals, although I bought one for the Rockefeller Collection and asked him if he would do some small paintings. Rojas, who is a very dignified man, thought this was a strange idea, but was willing to try. The only problem was that he couldn't think of subjects other than the *Basilica* or *La Virgen*, so I would suggest a kitchen, or the view across from his house, or a *vivienda* (the inner courtyard around which a group of families live), a market or a cemetery during the *Day of the Dead*. The paintings were done from 1978 to 1980.

Annie O'Neill

Plate 9 (top)
Jacinto Rojas, *Vivienda*, V-20-80, 48 x 32 inches.

Plate 10 (bottom)
Home and Hearth/Hogar y Fogon Installation View, University Art Museum, 1992.

Plate 11 (right)
Glazed Majolica Platter (Quanajuato, Quanajuato), early 1970s, 15 1/2 (dia.) x 2 3/4 inches (h.)

Plate 12, *Miniature Tableau*, 18 1/2 x 10 1/2 x 8 inches. This typical Mexican kitchen from the city of Puebla displays the world of popular art in miniature. A kitchen, after all, is really a small museum of handmade utilitarian pottery. The walls are decorated with loving arrangements of plates and casseroles, and the shelves are adorned with water jugs, pitchers, baskets, bowls, utensils, *molcajetes* and a variety of chocolate jars, beanpots and storage vessels. The kitchen is home to carved wooden spoon holders, a straw fan to fan the charcoal, and painted rush chairs. Highly glazed Talavera tiles decorate walls and ovens, and a diversity of copper pots and pans are always in use. Chickens or turkeys can be found wandering in a kitchen, a sleeping cat is curled in a corner, and it is not unusual to have other barnyard animals visiting. This kitchen even has a mariachi band serenading the inspired cook making a savory *Mole Poblano*.

Mexico's obsession with miniaturization reveals the simple pleasures small treasures give the young and the old who are young at heart. Miniatures serve to socialize the young through play. They are often the first pieces made by the children of artisans, and they are the objects most lovingly fashioned by artisans in a country enamored of toys and all things small and beautiful.

Plate 13
Home Altar Installation View, University Art Museum, 1992. Carved chest (Cuanajo, Michoacán), 30 x 48 x 18 inches; (left) retablo in tin and glass frame of *Crucifixion*; late 19th century, Central Mexico; various tin candlesticks (Mexico, D.F., Oaxaca, Oaxaca); (center, over chest) urban popular art mixed media construction of *Virgin of Guadalupe*; (right) tin retablo of *Face of Christ* (19th century central Mexico); (right wall) family photographs and religious pictures; (lower right) *Tree of Life* candelabra by Herón Martinez (see *Innovators*, Plate 32).

Home Altars and the Virgin of Guadalupe
In Mexico, religion permeates people's lives, and home altars are very common. Wax candles burn constantly in glass holders and natural or plastic flowers in abundance are placed on the altar. Each family adopts their own patron saint to ask for special protection. Favorite saints vary regionally, and in central Mexico, the most common are: *Santo Niño de Atocha*, a ten year old Christ with a staff in his hand, who has a Sanctuary in Plateros, Zacatecas; *San Martin Caballero* who offers his cloak to a poor man, the Sacred Heart (a Christ figure with a glowing heart), various closeups and depictions of Christ Himself and, of course, the Virgin of Guadalupe, *Patroness of Mexico and Empress of America*.

The best way to understand the impact of the Invasion of Mexico, especially that which is designated as its Spiritual Conquest, is the phenomenon that arises with the "miraculous" apparitions of the dark-skinned Virgin of Guadalupe to a humble Náhuatl layman, Juan Diego. Upon four successive apparitions at the top of the Tepeyac Hill, some 20 miles northeast of the heart of Mexico City, the Virgin of Guadalupe expressed her wish that a Sanctuary be built on the site for her veneration. The location was the same site where *Tonantzin* (Our Sacred Mother), was venerated prior to the Invasion. The acting archbishop, Fray Juan de Zumárraga immediately realized that this was an icon on which the Church could capitalize in order to reinforce the adoption of the new religion. The importance of the Virgin of Guadalupe to the culture of Mexico has not waned over the centuries.

Altares Familiares Y La Virgen De Guadalupe
La religiosidad permea la vida de las personas, y un altar familiar es muy común. Veladoras está prendidas permanentemente, flores naturales o de plástico son colocadas en grandes floreros. Cada familia escoge a los Santos y Vírgenes a quien le rezan y solicitan protección especial, en adición a los que se encuentran en la iglesia local y los santuarios. Las imágenes favoritas varian regionalmente, y en la parte central de México los mascomunes son: el Santo *Niño de Atocha*, un Christo-niño a los 10 años de edad, venerado en su santuario de Plateros, Zacatecas; *San Martin Cabellero*, que protege a los desposeidos al ofrecer su capa a un pobre; el Sagrado Corazón, una figura de Cristo con un corazón que brilla y tiene vida propia; varios acercamientos y representaciones de Cristo; y claro, está, la Virgen de Guadalupe, *Patrona de México y Emperatriz de América*.

La Major manera de comprender el impacto de la Conquista, especialmente aquello que ha venido a conocerse como la Invasion de México Espiritual, es el fenómeno que surgió a partir de las "milagrosas" apariciones de la Virgen de Guadalupe a un humilde campesino nahuatl, Juan Diego, Quien ya habia sido bautizado. Despues de 4 apariciones sobre el Cerro del Tepeyac, unos 32 kilómetros al noroeste del corazón de la ciudad de México, la Virgen de Guadalupe le expresó a Juan Diego que su deseo era que se le construyese un santuario en ese lugar para su veneración. En esa misma localidad se veneraba a *Tonantzin* o Nuestra Sagrada Madre, antes de la Invasion. El arzobispo en funciones, Fray Juan de Zumárraga inmediatamente aquilató que este era el icono que la Iglesia podria capitalizar para reforzar la adopción, y tuvo toda la razón! Su importancia e influencia no han disminuido a pesar de los siglos.

Plate 14
Installation View, University Art Museum, 1992.
Lacquered gourds; lacquered dowry chest by **Alfonso Jiménez** (Olinalá) 26 x 32 x 15 1/2 inches; rebozo (Hueyapan, Puebla). Painted chair (Tenancingo), 47 1/2 x 21 1/2 x 17 1/2 inches, on loan from Mr. and Mrs. James Wilson.

Dowry Chest

Five or more artisans work on one painted dowry chest. A carpenter makes the wooden chest from the highly fragrant *lináloe* wood harvested in the tropical areas of Guerrero. Various family members collect the minerals and make the oil and pigments. A woman generally performs the critical burnishing of the base coat. Polishing is performed by a specialist, and a painter completes the work.

Lacquerware is one of Mexico's most ancient crafts, and evidence of widespread pre-Hispanic Indian production is conclusive. When the Spaniards arrived in Mexico they were stunned by the brilliant and diverse selection of lacquerware they saw in the Aztec marketplaces. Olinalá, a small village in the rugged *Sierra Madre del Sur* of Guerrero, was and still is devoted to this labor intensive craft. The techniques of lacquerware have not changed significantly for hundreds of years.

The base material for Olinalá lacquer is an oil extracted from crushed and boiled chia seeds. After the first coat of oil and powdered dolomite is applied and burnished with the heel of the hand, layers of the oil and locally mined pigments are applied and polished, building up a very resistant base. This lacquered base can then be painted with paints that the 19th century artisans made with natural pigments. The traditional base colors are a deep orange-red or black. Two techniques are now practiced in Olinalá, *rayado* (incised), and *dorado* (painted) as seen in the chest (Plate 14). In the *rayado* technique, as seen in the gourds, the surface is given two coats of lacquer in contrasting colors. After the design is scratched into the lacquer with a thorn, needle or sharpened quill, the top coat is partially scraped away revealing the color below (Plate 15).

The craft was revived in the late 1920s, and the late Carlos Espejel was instrumental in reviving it once again in the late 1960s when the number of artisans had dwindled to seven. Lacquerware is now produced by most Olinalá households.

Lacquered Gourds

Gourds have been used and decorated by artisans throughout Mexican history. Their multitude of shapes has led to an equal variety of uses from the most logical and enduring water vessels and bowls to storage containers, hats, rattles and decorative objects. Lacquering is one of Mexico's oldest arts and fragments of colored gourds have been found in pre-hispanic tombs. Gourds are still used in many parts of Mexico as canteens and, when cut into a bowl shape, to hold hot drinks and gruel.

In Olinalá, Guerrero, artisans turn gourds into exquisite containers for sewing materials (Plate 14). Preparing a gourd so that it is dry and smooth enough to hold lacquer is a time consuming process. The base coat of oil, made from either chia seed oil or the fat from aje (obtained from a boiled insect), is covered by powdered dolomite and burnished. Then the ground pigments are applied and burnished to a brilliant sheen. The layer can be thin or it can be built up to produce a thick coat. Burnishing a gourd is extremely difficult because of its curved surface.

Plate 15
Damaso Ayala (Olinalá, Guerrero), *Lacquered Gourd* (detail of black cat on red ground), 1975.

Plate 16
Crane Wall Vase (Temalacacingo, Guerrero), ca. 1978, painted, lacquered gourd, 20 1/2 x 5 x 8 inches.

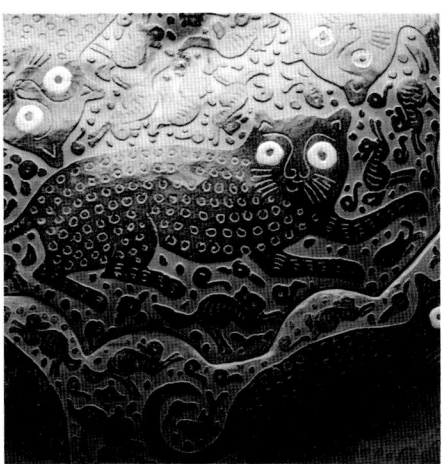

Plate 17
Installation View of Regional Costumes, University Art Museum, 1992.

Rebozo (on chair, Plate 14)
A *rebozo* is an indispensable part of the *mestiza* and Indian woman's wardrobe. It serves as a shawl, a baby carrier, a head covering, a support for a basket or water jug and is used in certain indigenous dances. It can be intricately woven in complex ikat patterns or coarsely woven of cotton or wool. In the 18th century it was stylish to embroider the surface with rural scenes. *Rebozos* were originally woven for *mestiza* women who would not dress like their Indian neighbors and yet couldn't afford Spanish finery. They have since been adopted for use by Indian women throughout Mexico.

In l976, I flew into Olinalá to work on photographs for a book about lacquerware. We visited Alfonso Jiménez who was working on an elaborate painted chest with a pastoral landscape on the front panel. It takes several weeks to paint a large chest. I noticed that on the door to the back room was an oil painting and was surprised to see that he had tacked the painting to the door frame. I asked if I could buy his door and he agreed.

The pastoral scene is a landscape of the mountainous approach to Olinalá. To reach the area a small plane must enter through a narrow opening in the surrounding mountains and if the wind is difficult cannot land. Jiménez painted an idealized landscape with all the elements real or wished for that take place around his village. Deer have been hunted out of the area, corn grows on the mountainside, fish are less abundant than in the old days and storks might fly by occasionally. It is curious that his painting has so many elements of the exquisite colonial lacquered chests. The eagle and serpent were often painted on 19th century chest panels, and the couple bringing corn in from the milpa were also a common motif. Storks were also a popular motif with overtones of fertility. Olinalátecos are still agriculturists and very much attached to their land in the remote Sierra Madre of Guerrerro.

Annie O'Neill

Plate 18
Alfonso Jiménez (Olinalá, Guerrero)
Olinalá Painting, ca. 1976
76 x 32 1/2 inches

Plate 19
Sampler, (mid 19th century, Central Mexico),
55 x 55 inches.
Mexican samplers are a compendium of stitchery and popular embroidery designs. This rare 19th century piece illustrates a wealth of motifs and techniques that were practiced by young Mexican convent girls under the tutelage of devout Spanish nuns. These highly skilled girls went on to adorn *servilletas* and clothing for clerics and the wealthy whose finery reflected their status. This large sampler is a veritable design inventory of the times, includes cross-stitch, herringbone, satin stitch, fish bone, stem and feather stitch, as well as a variety of drawn and gauze work. Many of these stitches and motifs are still popular in contemporary Indian costumes and embroidered pieces (Plate 17).

Plate # 20
Ceremonial Hupil from Magdalenas (Chiapas)
30 x 32 inches.
The *huipil*, a woman's tunic-like costume, called *huipili* by the Aztecs, is the most commonly worn garment in Indian Mexico. It is made by joining rectangular strips woven on a backstrap loom. The weave can vary from gauze-like fabric to tightly woven cotton. The surface can be adorned with intricate or simple embroidery in geometric or floral and animal motifs. The embroidery stitches include a great variety of techniques from simple cross stitch to elaborate brocading. These loose fitting garments are made for everyday use and for ceremonial occasions. A finely woven *huipil* is expected to last a lifetime and often is a symbol of status for the weaver.

Plate 21
Embroidery (Tenango de Doria, Hidalgo)
79 1/2 x 65 inches.

Plate 22
Embroidery (detail)

Embroidery

In the past twenty-five years the Otomí women of Tenango de Doria have transferred their embroidery skills from making satin stitched *servilletas* (tortilla warming cloths) that had been popular since the 19th century to producing elaborate multi-colored embroideries covered with a profusion of fantastic animals, birds, plants, devils, and imaginary figures incorporated with traditional motifs. Before the 19th century, women embroidered on hand-loomed sisal for altar cloths. The work and commercial success of Tenango de Doria embroideries has inspired the women of San Pablito, Puebla. These women also made the labor intensive bark paper which was sold to artisans in the state of Guerrero.

Innovators

During the last 40 years a number of folk artists have received particular recognition as *Innovators* and have been set apart from the rest of their fellow artisans. The recognition of that special "spark" that distinguishes the artist from the copyist has undoubtedly been an incentive and moving force for these exceptional individuals to continue their work. However, for some, success has also meant that they outgrow the traditional family structure and establish workshops that incorporate local hired labor. These assistants handle a line of production while the folk artist works on commissioned works and special pieces for juried competitions. For others this method of productivity has meant ostracism and even death because they challenge traditional political institutions.

Before external recognition evolved, the traditional mechanisms of recognition and prestige for the Mexican folk artist had been to specialize in ritual and ceremonial objects that demanded the best materials, the highest technical expertise, and great creativity to introduce subtle changes that were accepted and admired by the majority of the community.

Innovadores
Durante los últimos 40 años un número de artistas populares han sido señalados por su calidad de Innovadores, y han sido reconocidos y separados del resto de sus compañeros artesanos. El reconocimiento de esa "chispa" que distingue al artista del copista ha sido indudablemente un incentivo y detonador para que estos individuos excepcionales continúen su labor creativa. Sin embargo, para algunos, ese éxito ha significado que transforman la estructura familiar de producción en un taller con asalariados. Estos asistentes se encargan de una linea de producción mientras el Artista Popular trabaja piezas especiales para concursos o por encargo de coleccionistas y particulares. Para otros su éxito ha significado el rechazo de su comunidad y hasta la muerte porque enfrentan y retan a las formas tradicionales de poder.

Antes de que se desarrollara el reconocimiento externo, al seno de las comunidades un Artista Popular encontraba prestigio y trabajo realizando objetos rituales y ceremoniales, que demandaban los mejores materiales, la excelencia técnica y gran creatividad para introducir cambios sutiles que fueran aceptados y admirados por la mayoria de su comunidad.

Josefina Aguilar
Josefina Aguilar, an innovative craftswoman from Ocotlán de Morelos, Oaxaca reveals, popularizes and portrays village life with her small painted ceramic dolls. In the *Village Tableau*, Zapotecans bearing gifts are paying tribute to the Virgin of Guadalupe who is surrounded by church candles and angels. A couple, following their marriage, have come to leave flowers at the shrine. *Campesinos* further afield are relaxing, drinking and going to market where they can purchase pottery, baskets, animals, food and miniatures.

Throughout Mexico the marketplace is where people make weekly purchases or sell their goods. It is a time to socialize with friends, buy or sell an animal and catch up on regional news. In the Oaxaqueño markets many languages are spoken but Spanish is the common tongue. Animals are ever present, and an important part of Mexican life for thousands of years. They are beasts of burden, symbolic figures and food. In this tableau animals are represented in the forms of small and large bells—a successful innovation and hallmark of Aguilar's work.

Plate 23
Josefina Aguilar, *Village Tableau*, University Art Museum, 1992, 47 1/2 x 47 1/2 x 70 inches. Hand formed, single-fired painted earthenware figures by the Aguilar family Ocotlán de Morelos, Oaxaca. *(Tableau construction by John Ianelli, Studioworks, Voorheesville, New York.)*

Plate 24 (right)
Josefina Aguilar (Ocotlán de Morelos, Oaxaca), *Tehuana*, ca. 1970, hand formed, single-fired painted earthenware, 23 x 11 1/2 x 9 inches.

Plate 25 (opposite page)
Doña Teodora Blanco (Atzompa, Oaxaca), *Figure*, ca. 1970, single-fired earthenware, 26 x 8 1/2 x 8 1/2 inches.

Josefina Aguilar,
Josefina Aguilar, the daughter of utilitarian potters, is one of three sisters carrying on her family tradition of doll making. She no longer makes the traditional Ocatlán incense burners and small dolls, but concentrates on multi-figure sets that are a tableau of Mexican life: weddings, wakes, baptisms, nativities, markets and *Day of the Dead* scenes. She produces pieces for stores and tourists, and her work is highly acclaimed and awarded nationally and internationally. Her statuesque and stolid figures of Indians have a unique quality symbolizing the dignity, patience and reticence of rural Indians. This large ceramic doll is a *Tehuana*, a woman from the Isthmus of Tehuantepec. Aguilar is very experimental with clay and sensitive to the postures of her figures. *Rebozos* casually fall over shoulders, sarapes are securely clutched and rosaries carefully held. She spends the most time hand modelling the extraordinary faces of her dolls, trying to capture their spirit, fears, anguish, pride and dignity.

Doña Teodora Blanco
Teodora Blanco, one of the most unique and vital folk artists in Mexico, died in 1981, leaving behind a history of creative invention which set her apart from potters in Santa María Atzompa. Her parents were successful farmers as well as traditional potters and it was not necessary to push Teodora into commercial pottery. As a child she visited archaeological museums in Oaxaca and was inspired by animal and figural ceramics. She was also profoundly influenced not only by the forms of the water coolers from the San Blas Atempa on the Isthmus of Tehuantepec, but by their highly stylized faces which bear resemblance to certain ancient ceramics. The pinched and flattened faces, wide-eyed stares, dignified postures, and floral decorations of Teodora Blanco's dolls, the traditional Ocotlán dolls, and the San Blas Atempa water cooler bases, exhibit the transmission and adaptation of regional styles. Her innovations began in her teens when she created animal musicians. She then started attaching wings and tails to pitchers, whose spouts became animal heads. If she was working on a traditional Atzompa form, she would always add appendages of animals.

In her late twenties she began making her legendary female figures. These figures constantly evolved and changed, from her original market figures to her experimentations with various combinations of women, animals and mythical creatures. Beasts poked out of abdomens, breasts became animal heads, and animals and babies pulled at shoulders and skirts. Her later pieces illustrate her belief in *nahuales*, a pre-Hispanic concept that each person has a particular animal counterpart that from birth protects and befriends. Her preoccupation with nurturing and the intermingling of animal and human spirits was a dominant theme in her later pieces—pieces that displayed a baroque flair for decoration. Her impulse for surface adornment was intense, and by the late 1970s the entire front of the figure was covered with appliqued coils, animals emerging from the body, and arms always engaged in holding or carrying children, animals or market baskets. In spite of this sculptural abandon, her figures of women are dignified and elegant.

Teodora Blanco, una de las artistas populares mas vitales y singulares de México murió en 1981, dejando una historia de creatividad que la hizo sobresalir del resto de los alfareros de Santa María Atzompa. Sus padres fueron agricultores exitosos, e igualmente alfareros tradicionales, así que no tuvo la necesidad de entrar a la alfarería comercial. De niña visitó los museos arqueológicos de Oaxaca, inspirándose en los animales y la cerámica figurativa. No solo la influenciaron las formas de las enfriaderas de agua de San Blas Atempa en el Istmo de Tehuantepec, sino tambien sus rostros altamente estilizados que asemejan cierta cerámica pre-hispánica. Las caras pellizcadas y planas, con grandes ojos de mirada fija, postura dignificada y decoraciones florales de las figuras de Teodora Blanco, las muñecas tradicionales de Ocotlán, y las bases enfriadoras de San Blas Atempa, muestran la transmisión y adaptación de estilos regionales. Sus innovaciones comenzaron de adolescente cuando creó animales mùsicos. De allí comenzó a agregarle alas y colas a las jarras, cuyas bocas se convertían en cabezas de animales. Si tomaba una forma tradicional, siempre le agregaría un detalle de animales.

Entre los 25 y 30 años de edad comenzó a hacer sus legendarias figuras de mujeres. Constantemente cambiaban y evolucionaban, desde sus clásicas placeras, a su experimentación con varias combinaciones de mujeres, animales y criaturas mitológicas. Bestias que se asomaban del abdomen, senos que se convertían en cabezas de animales, y animales y bebés que jalaban de los hombros y las faldas. Sus piezas posteriores muestran su creencia en los *nahuales*, un antiguo concepto en que cada persona, desde su nacimiento, tiene un animal compañero que se le acerca y lo protege. La preocupación por mezclar y propiciar a los espiritus humanos y animales dominó en sus ùltimas piezas—piezas que mostraban un sentido barroco de la decoración—.Su impulso para llenar la superficie con adornos era intenso, y para finales de los '70 todo el frente de las figuras se recubre de pastillaje, animales emergiendo del cuerpo, y brazos cargando niños, animales o canastos del mercado. A pesar de este arrebato escultórico, sus figuras femeninas son siempre dignas y elegantes. Para Teodora sólo había una razón para vivir: la alfarería.

Plate 26
Heriberto Castillo (Izúcar de Matamoros, Puebla), *Turtle with Figures and Mermaid*, ca. 1970, single-fired painted and varnished earthenware, 5 x 6 x 11 inches.

The Castillo family are Izúcar's other innovators. They have departed from traditional forms and create elaborate stacked figures. Their inventive constructions are delicate and humorous.

Plate 27
Aurelio Flores (Izúcar de Matamoros, Puebla), *Tree of Life Censor*, ca.1970, single-fired, painted and varnished earthenware, 26 3/4 x 20 x 7 1/2 inches.

Aurelio Flores

Aurelio Flores lived his entire life in Izúcar de Matamoros, a village of traditional potters south of the great ceremonial center of Cholula. Izúcar is known for ceremonial incense burners and elaborate *Trees of Life* that are covered with a creamy gesso and then painted with analine dyes covered with a shiny natural varnish. Flores expanded his production creating decorative figures and elaborate *Trees of Life*. It was Aurelio Flores' work that inspired other communities of potters to turn their traditional pieces into elaborate *Trees of Life* and *Trees of Death* and to create decorative work based on biblical themes.

Aurelio Flores vivió y murió en Izúcar de Matamoros, Puebla, un pueblo alfarero tradicional, al sur del gran centro ceremonial do Cholula, y culturalmente parte de Acatlán. La raíz de su inspiración fue la alfarería ritual policroma, compuesta por incensarios y candeleros con la gifura de San Miguel. Al igual que muchos de los otros innovadores, su trabajo evolucionó hacia lo decorativo y escultórico. Quizás fue el trabajo de este artesano lo que constituyó el origen de los *Arboles de la Vida*, derivados de los candeleros para la iglesia, a los cuales se agregaron *Arboles de la Muerte*, y temas biblicos.

Manuel Jimenez

These brightly painted wooden animals (Plate 28, opposite page) were made in the late 1960s to 1980 by Manuel Jiménez, a former adobe mason and bracero cane cutter, who started carving for his own pleasure. By the mid 1970s he had enormous influence on carving in the Oaxaca valley. Jiménez recalls that as a small boy he loved tending animals and out in the fields he would often fashion small figures from stream bed mud. These small toys were the beginning of his art. When he began carving wood there was little call for his work aside from an occasional need for a mask or a *santo* in his village. He took his earliest pieces to a vendor in the Oaxaca market and soon tourist shops discovered him. Jiménez uses *tsompanclé* wood from the surrounding mountains. He carves the pieces when the wood is green and soft, using a machete for roughing out the animal and a knife for fine carving. Chisels, awls, rasps and drills simplify his production. With an economy of machete stokes he manages to transform a branch into an engaging animal. In addition to animals he carves large Nativity figures, sirens, madonnas and devils. His highly acclaimed carvings are collected nationally and internationally. His success has stimulated entire villages in the Oaxaca valley to produce carvings for resale to tourists.

Manuel Jiménez

Oriundo de Arrazola, Oaxaca, las figuras de animales de madera pintados en colores brillantes (Foto 28), fueron producidos desde finales de los '60 hasta 1980, por un ex-albañil de adobe y bracero cortador de caña, que se inició en la talla de madera por gusto. Para mediados de los años '70 ejercía una enorme influencia en la talla de madera del valle de Oaxaca. Jimenez recuerda que de niño le encantaba pastorear y cuidar a los animales y cuando salía a los campos, frecuentemente modelaba pequeñas figuras del lodo de los arroyos. El considera que estos pequeños juguetes hechos de niño fueron el inicio de su arte. Cuando empezó a tallar la madera, no habia mayor demanda para su trabajo más allá de una máscara o un santo para su pueblo. Llevó algunas de sus primeras figuras a un marchante en el mercado de Oaxaca y rápidamente fué descubierto por las tiendas para turistas. Jimenez usa la madera de tzompantle que se dá en las montañas aledañas. Talla las piezas cuando aùn está verde y suave la madera, usando un machete para marcar la figura y un cuchillo para los detalles finos. Hoy en día usa cincel, punzón, taladro, y rallador. Con unos cuantos machetazos logra transformar una rama en un animal simpático con energía abundante. Además de animales también talla grandes figuras de Belenes, sirenas, madonnas y diablos (incluídos en la exposición). Sus tallas altamente aclamadas son coleccionadas internacionalmente y su éxito individual le ha brindado un modo de vida a pueblos enteros del valle de Oaxaca que hacen figuras para los turistas. Las figuras humanas que están incluídas son las ùnicas que el artesano talló antes de dedicarse por completo a tallar animales.

Pedro Linares

Pedro Linares, Mexico's foremost *cartonero*, was a legendary and innovative artisan who died in 1992 at almost 90. The *cartonero* soaks torn paper bags, old newspapers, or wrapping paper until it is pulpy and pliable. With the addition of wheat flour and casein, he presses the mixture into or onto molds that are covered with beeswax. After drying, the paper is cut and removed from the mold and then rejoined before being intricately painted. As a young man he worked with his father, a *cartonero*, making little masks, *piñatas* and Judas figures (Plate 59) for seasonal fiestas. During a serious illnesss more than 40 years ago, Linares had a death bed vision in which he saw ugly and frightening things—ominous clouds in the shape of dragons with sharp teeth and protruding eyes, hurling themselves at him. From this experience, *alebriges* were born. In the 1960s he transformed his death bed vision, coupled with his skill as a *cartonero*, into exuberant paper monsters that were intricately painted and wildly outlandish—flying dragons, winged lizards and mythical creatures that leap and soar in a world of ultimate fantasy. It is very likely that Linares saw a Posada engraving portraying the seven deadly sins as flying winged creatures. Linares was fascinated with the endless artistic potential of this subject and was able to implement his seasonal production of *piñatas*, Judas figures, devils, demons and skeletons which allowed him to work full time as an artisan. His sons and grandsons now carry on the work he began. Pedro Linares was the 1990 recipient of the *National Award for the Arts and Sciences* (México).

Pedro Linares, el cartonero mas famoso de México, fué un legendario e innovador artesano que murió en 1992 a los casi 90 años de edad. De joven comenzó a trabajar con su padre, un cartonero,

realizando pequeñas máscaras, Piñatas y Judas (Foto 59) para la quema en Semana Santa, el Dia de Muertos y fiestas estacionales. Durante una grave enfermedad, Linares tuvo una visiones de muerte, en las que vió horribles y espantosas criaturas—nubes de mal agüero en forma de dragones con dientes filosos y ojos saltones, aventándose hacia él. De este viaje al más allá nacieron los alebrijes, y comenzó una producción importante en los '60. Transformó su visión de muerte, junto con su habilidad como cartonero, en monstruos de papel exhuberantes, que eran pintados meticulosamente y caprichosamente extravagantes—dragones voladores, lagartijas aladas y criaturas mitológicas que saltan y se elevan en un mundo de total fantasía.

Es mas probable que Linares, un cartonero por oficio, hubiera visto un grabado de Posada mostrando los siete pecados capitales como criaturas aladas que atacan a un hombre rico que murió víctima de sus propios vicios. A Linares le fascinaba el potencial artístico infinito de este tema, y logró combinarlo con su producción de temporada de piñatas, figuras de Judas, diablos, demonios y calacas, lo que le permitía trabajar como artesano de tiempo completo. Sus hijos y nietos continùan con el trabajo que él dejó.

El cartón es un arte para la era del reciclaje. El cartonero remoja pedazos de bolsas de papel, periódicos viejos, y papel de envoltura hasta que se convierte en una pulpa flexible. Al agregarle harina de trigo y caseína pega la mezcla dentro o sobre los moldes que están cubiertos de cera de abeja. Después de secarse, se saca el papel del molde y se vuelve a unir antes de ser pintado profusamente.

Plate 28
Manuel Jiménez (Arrazola, Oaxaca), *Animals* (detail of installation), ca. 1970, painted wood.

Plate 29
Pedro Linares (Mexico D.F.), *Alebriges*, papier-mâché, paint and varnish, 18 x 19 1/2 x 17 1/2 inches.

Candelario Medrano

Candelario Medrano, an innovator from Santa Cruz de las Huertas, Jalisco, was one of Mexico's best known folk ceramists. As a young man he apprenticed to Julio Acero, the outstanding artisan in Santa Cruz, but until Medrano was fifty, he gathered firewood for potters and made small whistles to sell at fiestas. It was Jorge Wilmot, the great Tonala designer, potter and innovator who studied all over the world, who encouraged Medrano to put his little whistle figure on an ark. His repertory soon expanded from Noah's Ark, to include buses, airplanes, trains and multi-tiered houses, covered with groups of people. His surrealistic and fanciful animals were a later development and based on the supernatural, local customs, beliefs and mythologies incorporated with elements of stories told to him by his grandparents. With all his international success he never made more money than he did as a woodcutter, and his serious drinking problem led to ill health and finally death.

Candelario Medrano, un innovador de Santa Cruz de las Huertas, Jalisco, fué uno de los ceramistas populares mexicanos mejor conocidos. De joven fue aprendiz de Julio Acero el artesano mas renombrado de Santa Cruz, sin embargo hasta que Medrano cumplió cincuenta años de edad, se dedicó a recolectar leña para los alfareros y a elaborar pequeños silbatos para vender en las fiestas. Fué Jorge Wilmot, el extraordinario diseñador, ceramista e innovador de Tonalá que estudió por todo el mundo, quien animó a Medrano a que colocara su silbatito sobre un arca. Pronto su repertorio creció de un Arca de Noé a camiones, aviones, trenes y casas de muchos pisos, todos recubiertos con grupos de gentes. Los animales surrealistas e imaginativos fueron un desarrollo posterior, nutridos por costumbres, creencias y mitos de lo sobrenatural, mezclados con historias que le habían contado sus abuelos. Con todo y su éxito internacional nunca hizo mas dinero de lo que había logrado como leñador, y su problema serio de alcoholismo lo llevaron a la muerte.

Plate 30
Candelario Medrano (Santa Cruz de las Huertas, Jalisco), *Airplane*, 1975, single-fired and varnished earthenware, 33 x 27 x 14 inches.

Plate 31
Candelario Medrano, *Animal grouping*, early 1970s, single-fired and varnished earthenware: Rooster (11 x 5 3/4 x 7 inches); Man and Náhuatl (10 1/4 x 11 x 7 inches); Fox (12 x 5 x 4 1/2 inches).

Plate 32
Herón Martinez (Acatlán de Osorio, Puebla), *Tree of Life*, single-fired earthenware, burnished with river stones, 32 x 24 x 8 inches. (Plate 13, Home Altar Installation.)

Plate 33
Herón Martinez, hand painted pottery, 12 x 12 x 5 inches. This is an example of his esrly style.

Herón Martinez

Herón Martinez, mastercraftsman from Acatlán, Puebla, died on November 4, 1990 at age 72. He was one of the few craftsmen who was able to gain recognition both at home and abroad due to a fortuitous combination of very hard work and creative genius. The son and nephew of utilitarian potters, Herón initially shunned his inherited trade and dabbled at odd jobs for six years before returning to Acatlán and dedicating himself to what he knew best—pottery. As early as 1947 researchers from the Museum of Anthropology in Mexico City recognized his talent and mounted an exhibit, bringing his work to the attention of German, French and American dealers and collectors. In 1974 his work was included in the great World Crafts Council exhibit *In Praise of Hands* in Toronto, Canada. Herón's style evolved from his rediscovery of local prehispanic pot shards, finely burnished and slip-decorated with geometric forms, techniques he loved, continually perfected and embellished. He created polychrome painted figures, which evolved into giant trees of life, such as the Creation, Noah's Art, and the Nativity of Christ. In his later years he produced fanciful insects, animals, ducks and complex trees of life in highly burnished natural clay.

Herón Martinez, Maestro Artesano de Acatlán, Puebla, murio el pasado 4 de noviembre de 1990 a la edad de 72 años, uno de los pocos artesanos que logró grandes reconocimientos tanto en su pais como en el exterior. En el se conjugaron fortuitamente el arduo trabajo y el genio creador. Hijo y nieto de alfareros de objetos utilitarios, Herón inicialmente rechazó su oficio heredado y se dedicó a varios trabajos como albañil y peón de carretera durante 6 años, antes de regresar a Acatlán en 1946 para retomar aquello que conocía bien: la alfareria. Ya en 1947 fue descubierto por investigadores del Museo de Antropología de la ciudad de México, quienes montaron una exposicíon de su obra. De allí en adelante su trabajo llamó poderosamente la atensión de colleccionistas y comerciantes alemanes, americanos y franceses, y culminó con su representación de México en la gran exposición *In Praise of Hands*, que se llevó a cabo en Toronto, Canadá en 1974, patrocinada por el Consejo Mundial de Artesanias (WCC). El estilo particular de Herón se desarrolló a partir de su redescubrimiento de restos arqueológicos de su región, finamente bruñidas y decoradas con motivos geométricos en engobe. Estas dos técnicas las empleó siempre, perfeccionándolas continuamente. Tambien pasó por una época de pintado policromado, de elaboración de animales y piezas fantásticas, y el desarrollo de gigantes Arboles de la Vida con motivos religiosos como La Creación, El Arca de Noé, El Nacimiento de Cristo, y otros.

Isaac Vasquez, Master Weaver
Isaac Vasquez of Teotitlán del Valle, a Zapotec village in the valley of Oaxaca, has emerged as a master weaver in a weaving village that has been closely attuned to the whims of a tourist market for the last thirty years. The Zapotecs have a textile tradition dating to the late 15th century and began weaving wool soon after the Spaniards introduced sheep to Mexico. The market for sarapes was always within Mexico, although we know that in the 1930s Teotitlán was selling to tourists. The Bracero program of the 1950s exposed the villagers to North American culture and gave them money for business investments and entreprenurial activity. The opening of the Pan-American highway passing only miles from Teotitlán, enabled more intensive tourism.

Vasquez has chosen to carry on the traditional techniques of weaving using all wool weft yarns and hand dyeing with natural dyes. He works with his large extended family on all aspects of production from carding and spinning to the final weaving, rather than farming out his work. His designs are inspired by pre-Hispanic flat stamps and motifs from sites throughout Mexico. His sarapes are a compendium of ancient geometric, naturalistic and fantastic human, plant and animal symbolism interpreted with a sensitivity and color sense that few weavers possess.

Isaac Vasquez, Maestro Tejedor
Isaac Vasquez de Teotitlán del Valle, un pueblo zapoteco en el valle de Oaxaca, ha surgido como un maestro tejedor de un pueblo de tejedores armonizado desde hace treinta años a las exigencias de un mercado turístico. La tradición textil de los zapotecos se inicia a finales del siglo XV, y comenzaron a tejer lana cuando los Españoles introdujeron los borregos a México. El mercado para sarapes siempre fue nacional, aunque sabemos que en los años '30 ya estaban vendiendo a turistas. El programa de Braceros de los años '50 lo puso en contacto con la cultura de E.U.A. y le dió dinero en efectivo para iniciar pequeños negocios y empresas. El paso de la carretera Panamericana a unos cuantos kilómetros de Teotitlán tambien atrajo mas turismo.

Vasquez aplica la técnica tradicional de tejido usando hilos de la trama de lana pura, tiñiendo manualmente con tintes naturales. En vez de dar a maquilar, trabaja con su gran familia extensa para todas las fases de la producción, desde el cardado y el hilado hasta el tejido final. Sus diseños están inspirados en los sellos prehispánicos que se encuentran por todos los sitios arqueológicos de México. Sus sarapes resumen motivos geométricos y símbolos de animales, plantas y figuras humanas realistas e imaginarias, interpretados con un colorido y una sensibilidad que pocos tejedores poseen.

Plate 34
Isaac Vasquez, *Serpent*, ca. 1972, woolen tapestry, 58 x 38 inches.
This weaving by Teotitlán del Valle's master weaver depicts a serpent whose body incorporates the stepped fret design from the nearby ruins of Mitla. This weaving was made on a large treadle-loom with hand-carded, hand-spun and dyed wool. The spinning is done by Señora Vasquez who spins in the pre-Hispanic way using a spindle and a wooden shaft weighted with a clay spindle whorl. The natural dyes are made from local plants, leaves, bark, twigs, flowers, lichens and seeds.

Plate 35
Isaac Vasquez, *Contemporary Woven Codice*, ca. 1975, woolen tapestry, 82 x 44 1/2 inches.

Popular Arts in Transition: New Art Forms and Old Traditions

Many Mexican artisans and communities of artisans have realized that in order to survive in a rapidly changing world, it is necessary to adapt their traditional objects to consumers' needs. The second half of the 20th century has seen less expensive industrial goods replace utilitarian and ceremonial objects in the local markets. Collectors and government sponsored development programs based in cosmopolitan centers in North America and Europe, esteem the profound relationship these folk artists establish between their materials and their spirit. The creative ways in which folk artists transmit a particular vision of the world with humor, whim, and technical expertise is also valued.

The range of changes encompasses a large cross-section of ceramists, weavers, embroiderers, rag doll makers, painters, wood and bone carvers, and papier-mâché sculptors. Mexican artisans depict solemn *fiestas* and celebrations, myths and beliefs in hundreds of different ways. Their artistic output is mostly figurative, always enhanced with a touch of the fantastic. The artisans' trend has been to embellish, to exaggerate, to become more *baroque*, that is, to outdo oneself over and over again. And in this new context the anonymous artist, once considered a part of the definition of Folk Art, is replaced by a new generation of highly recognized folk artists who sign their works, show in specialized galleries and find their way into museums and international exhibitions. In addition, some communities that once had only a handful of artisans have seen the demand for their work rise to such a degree that whole villages now depend on craft production for their livelihood.

El Arte Popular en Transicion: Nuevas Formas y Antiguas Tradiciones
Muchos artesanos Mexicanos y comunidades artesanales se han dado cuenta que para sobrevivir en un mundo en rápida transformación, es necesario adaptar sus objetos tradicionales a las necesidades de un nuevo consumidor. La segunda mitad del siglo XX ha sido testigo de la sustitución de los objetos utilitarios y ceremoniales en los mercados locales, por objetos industrialmente elaborados con menor costo. Coleccionistas de centros cosmopolitas de Norteamérica y Europa, y programas gubernamentales de desarrollo han venido a reconocer la relación que establecen los artistas populares entre sus materiales y su espiritú. Tambien valoran las formas creativas con las que los artistas populares transmiten una visión particular del mundo con humor, ingenio y excelencia técnica.

Dentro de los cambios que han experimentado las artesanias, estas abarcan una muestra representativoa de alfareros, tejedoras, boardadoras, fabricantes de muñecas de trapo, pintores, talladores de madera y hueso, y escultores en papel y cartón. Los artesanos Mexicanos muestran en cientos de maneras diferentes sus celebraciones y *Fiestas* solemnes, y sus mitos y creencias. Mas que nada se han enfocado en un Arte Figurativo, siempre con un toque de lo fantástico, en una tendencia estética hacia la exageración, hacia lo *barroco*: el artista popular se forza a no repetirse a sí mismo. Y en este nuevo contexto el artista anónimo, una vez considedrado la esencia de la definición de Arte Popular, es reemplazado por una nueva generación de artistas populares que firman sus obras, exhiben en galerias de arte expecializadas y en museos, y tambien son objeto de libros y catálogos. Además, en no pocas comunidades, donde antes trabajaban unas cuantas familias, la demanda ha hecho que todo el pueblo dependa ahora de la producción artesanal parasu ingreso.

AMATE

Amate is the Náhuatl term for the paper made from pounding strips of bark from the *ficcus sp* tree until it meshes into a uniform surface. Before the Spanish Invasion, many codices, or sacred books, were made from this bark. Thousands of sheets were used by the Aztecs to make headdresses and strips that were dipped in hot rubber and ritually burned.

Since the Invasion only one Otomí village, San Pablito Pahuatlán in the State of Puebla, has continued to use it for ritual purposes. In the late 1950s, the owners of a folk art gallery in Mexico City suggested to Náhuatl pottery makers in the state of Guerrero (500 miles away from San Pablito) to start painting their bird and animal motifs on bark paper, supplied by the Otomís. The consequence of this suggestion has had a far-reaching impact on both regions: the deforestation and destruction of *amate* trees. The producers now turn to other bark species in their increasing dependence on the production of sheets of paper for these paintings sold to tourists. In addition, thousands of families from the Guerrero villages of Xalitla, Maxela, Oapan, and Ameyaltepec have now become more and more dependent on the sale of bark paintings, painted wooden fish and painted pottery for income.

Amate es el término en nahuatl para el papel de corteza de árbol que se elabora machacando tiras del árbil de la especie *ficcus sp* hasta formar una superficie plana. Previa a la Invasión Española, mucho Códices o libros sagrados fueron elaborados con esta fibra. Además miles de hojas eran usadas por los Aztecas para tocados y ropa ritual, en tiras cuyas puntas eran immersas en hule caliente y despues quemadas ritualmente.

Despues de la Invasión un solo pueblo otomi, San Pablito Pahuatlán en el estado de Puebla, conservó su uso ritual hasta nuestros dias. Al final de la década de los 1950, los dueños de una galeria de Arte Popular de la ciudad de México, le sugirieron a los alfareros nahuas del estado de Guerrero, distante unos 800 kilómetros de San Pablito, que pintaran sus diseños de pájaros y animales sobre papel de amate, hecho especialmente por los otomis. Este fue el inicio de una historia que ha tenido un impacto permanente en las dos regiones: la deforestación, hizo que los productores buscaran otras especies de maderas con cortezas, y además volverse mas dependientes de la producción y venta de hojas de papel. Y en el otro extremo, miles de familias de los pueblos de Xalitla, Maxela, Oapan y Ameyaltepec en Guerrero tambien se volvieron mas y mas dependientes de la venta de sus pinturas sobre corteza, de pescados de madera pintados y de cerámica pintada.

Plate 36
Figure, Amate, 30 x 7 x 7 inches

Plate 37 (upper)
Untitled, ca. 1970, Amate painting,
19 1/2 x 25 inches.

Plate 38 (lower)
Untitled, ca. 1970, Amate painting, .
24 x 18 inches

Plate 39 (opposite page)
Emilio de la Rosa (Ameyaltepec, Guerrero)
Amate painting, ca. 1970. 15 1/2 x 72 inches each

Plate 40 (frontispiece, inside cover)
Telesforo Rodriguez (Ameyaltepec, Guerrero),
Fiesta, ca. 1975, bark painting, 32 x 46 inches.
From field to fiesta, this oversized bark painting illustrates the world of a Nahua villager. This unusual composition incorporates ceremonial, agricultural and utilitarian elements of village life in Ameyaltepec, Guerrero. An elaborate *castillo* (fireworks tower) is in the process of its spectacular eruption, while women are still adorning it with firecrackers. Above the castillo, pulque enthusiasts are engaged in a variety of activities from a rousing fight to hauling cases of the potent drink to a fiesta behind a village band that is playing for participants in a bullfight. On the lower right, farmers are returning from tending their milpas (cornfields). The painting illustrates the diversity of bags, baskets and clothing carried and worn by men and women. It is also a sampler of the common plants found in the Rio Balsas countryside. Rodriguez has painted a variety of cactus, maguey and corn as well as flowers. Many sheets of thin bark were pounded together to make this unusually large and fine piece of San Pablito paper.

Plate 41
Mexican Dance Costumes
(left to right) Dance of *Chinelos* (Tepotzlan, Morelos); *Quetzales* (Cuetzalan, Puebla); *Matachines* (El Refugio, Zacatecas); *Viejitos* (Patzcuaro area of Michoacán); *Concheros*; *Negritos* (Sierra de Puebla). Collection of Pilar Gomez.

Plate 42
Masks, installation view, University Art Museum, Univerity at Albany.
upper shelf (left to right): **Erazmo Lopez** (La Floreda, Sinaloa), *Mexican Dance Mask* (Revolutionary Soldier), goat hide with cardboard cap; *Ceramic Mold* (Celaya, Queretaro), ca. 1940, used for papier-mâché monkey masks; *Toro Mask*, hide, mirror, paint and carved horns; *Monkey Mask*, wood, hair, teeth. Collection of Mr. and Mrs. Eugene Walter.
lower shelf (left to right)
Cora *Semana Santa Masks* (Jesus Maria, Nayarit), painted papier-mâché, ca. 1979. Collection of Pilar Gomez. *Mexican Helmut Mask* (Axoxuca, Guerrero), carved horns, painted rawhide and wood. Collection of Mr. and Mrs. Eugene Walter.

Plate 43
Mayo Indian Masks (*The Mayo Indians are a semi-nomatic tribe related to the North American Apache Indians.*)
(left) *Pascola Dance Mask*, carved by Saturnino Valenzuela (San Jose Rios, Rio Fuertes region), painted wood with goat hair. (right) *Goat Mask* - carved by Andres Valenzuela (Camajoa, Rio Guertes region), painted wood with goat hair. Collection of Mr. and Mrs. Eugene Walter.

Plate 44
Jaguar Mask (Guerrero), ca. 1940, carved and painted wood. Collection of Mr. and Mrs. Eugene Walter.

Plate 45 (above)
Fiesta Tableau, fireworks figures, 12 1/2 x 5 1/2 x 5 1/2 inches, fireworks, 20 x 6 x 6 inches

Plate 46 (right)
Torita (Tilcajete, Oaxaca), carved and painted wood, ca. 1975, 10 x 4 x 10 1/2 inches (detail of *Fiesta Tableau*).

Plate 47
Fiesta Tableau, dolls in regional costumes,
37 x 37 x21 inches

Festivals
Mexicans celebrate throughout the year—their festivals, *fiestas* and processions are among the world's most elaborate. These special occasions often culminate with a spectacular display of fireworks. At the center of all the activity is the *torito*, or little bull, carried atop the head of the firework maker. He cavorts with the group delighting, terrifying and mesmerizing as the fireworks on the bull explode. The crowd is made up of spectators, old and young, who often travel days from remote villages to attend the *fiesta*, listen to music, eat sweets and watch the dances. In this tableau we have a multi-cultural crowd of dolls made by artisans who in their traditional seasonal crafts are presenting themselves to others. There are regional cloth dolls of Indians from the Oaxaca Valley and surrounding mountains; *fiesta* participants and dancers from Patzcuaro, Michoacán; wooden *campesino* dolls from Oaxaca; woven palm leaf *charros* and a *charrita* from Puebla; a wooden *torito* from Oaxaca, a fireworks maker from Guerrero, a Lacandon couple from Chiapas and others.

La Fiesta
Los mexicanos celebran todo el año—sus festivales, fiestas y procesiones están dentro de las mas fastuosas del mundo. Estas ocasiones especiales generalmente culminan con una espectacular muestra de juegos pirotécnicos. Al centro de toda la actividad está el "torito", cargado sobre las cabeza del pirotécnico, quien juega con los espectadores, deleitando, asustando y hechizando mientras truenan los cohetes del torito. La multitud la conforman los viejos y jóvenes quienes llegan a viajar varios días desde comunidades lejanas para asistir a la fiesta, escuchar mùsica, comer dulces y ver las danzas.

Retablos

Retablos are religious paintings on tin, copper or canvas that are hung in churches to honor a particular saint. It is a tradition that goes back to Colonial times and includes representations of saints in the clothing of their time and order along with the various attributes associated with their lives and transition into sainthood. They are found in churches, chapels, and home altars throughout Mexico. *Retablos* are usually commissioned works, so the style of painting can vary widely. In the most remote villages these images of revered saints can be found surrounded by candles and flowers.

Plate 48
El Niño de Atocha Retablo, 7 x 10 inches.
El Niño de Atocha, one of the most common folk *retablo* themes, is a popular manifestation of the young Christ. This image had its origin in Atocha, Spain during the Moorish invasion. The tyrannical Moors, so the story is told, forbade anyone except for young children from visiting the incarcerated Christians on errands of mercy. The prisoners were starving and the *Atochans* prayed fervently for their deliverance. When a young child arrived dressed as a pilgrim carrying a staff, a water gourd, and a basket of food, their prayers were answered. Miraculously, there was still food in his basket and water in the gourd even after all the prisoners were fed. The *Niño's* attributes are consistant in *retablos*: a brimmed hat with a plume, a pilgrim's staff, a gourd, shafts of wheat, and a basket containing flowers or bread. *El Niño de Atocha* is the patron to whom people pray for the freeing of prisoners, for protection from physical violence, and for deliverance and rescue from serious dangers encountered during travel.

Plate 49 *Guadalupe and Widow*, 1858, painted ex-voto on tin, 7 1/8 x 10 1/8 inches.

Ex-votos

Ex-votos are small commissioned works on tin painted to commemorate recovery from an illness or escape from serious danger because of the miraculous intervention of a holy being. The *ex-voto* are divided into two parts, a charming and pictorial representation of the occurrence and the divine intervener, and an accompanying narrative and devotional text. These paintings are placed in churches by the recovered or saved in gratitude for the miraculous and divine powers that came to their assistance. In the 19th century great quantities of these small paintings were executed by unknown, untrained and often itinerant folk artists. They interpreted textual material into a dramatic rendition of an event. Tin was the chosen material replacing the canvas used earlier for *ex-votos* commissioned by the wealthy. Devotees placed these small pieces on the altar honoring the saint whose intervention is documented and commemorated in the painting. This custom arrived with the Spanish and was immediately adopted by wealthy Mexicans. After independence from Spain it was embraced by all. In many churches throughout central Mexico, walls are covered with hundreds of *ex-votos* offering a comprehensive glimpse not only of personal devotion and the power of religious personages but also of the social history and faith and dreams of the populace.

Plate 50 *Operation*, 1956, painted ex-voto on tin, 7 1/8 x 9 5/8 inches.

Milagros

The tin box houses a collection of nineteenth and twentieth century silver and metal milagros (miracles). These small pieces, in use since the sixteenth century, are hung in churches as offerings to revered saints in gratitude for a cure, a recovery, or a miraculous change in a difficult situation. The world of arms, legs, hands, eyes, huaraches, women's heads, barnyard animals and praying figures are common subjects for a silversmith. From the sixteenth to the early twentieth century, milagros were commissioned by the thankful and made by local silversmiths. The scope of subject matter could then extend to any situation. But, today these tiny treasures are rarely made by hand and no longer commissioned. They are cast in metal and then sewn onto a colorful ribbon ready to hand in church. Vendors of milagros stand outside churches and sell the appropriate "miracle" to the devout and thankful. In gratitude it is placed beside hundreds of others inside the church near the appropriate saint. Although the scope of subject matter no longer has the curious diversity, and the hand crafting has disappeared, the sentiment still persists.

Plate 51
Tin case with milagros, 7 1/2 x 14 x 2 inches.

Ceremonial Objects: Form and Symbol

Ceremonial objects and religious celebrations preserve their identity as long as they are used in ritual context. The driving force of the culture can be summed up in the concept of *Ofrenda*, or offering. *Fiestas* as collective celebrations are just that; each incense burner, votive candle and floral wreath, each group of dancers who has made a promise to the Saint, each cargoholder and his helpers who finance the *fiesta* and the whole pueblo or village work as participant/spectator to insure community and individual prosperity.

In ceremonial folk art objects, symbols determine forms. Profoundly religious aspects are captured in dance costumes, masks, incense burners and candle holders in the concept of Heaven and Hell and the *Day of the Dead* figures. They also are one of the representations of a well defined annual Fiesta calendar, deeply rooted in the agricultural cycle of corn, and the Saints that substituted the ancient Gods to whom one prays for successful crops and family protection.

Objetos Ceremoniales: Forma y Simbolo

Los objetos ceremoniales y las celebraciones religiosas conservan su identidad en la medida que son realizadas dentro del contexto ritual. La fuerza motriz de la cultura puede resumirse en el concedpto de la *Ofrenda*. Las *Fiestas* en tanto celebraciones colectivas son precisamente eso: cada incensario, cada vela votiva y arreglo floral, cada grupo de danzantes que ha hecho una plegaria al Santo, cada mayordomo (o carguero) y sus asistentes que patrocinan la *fiesta*, y todo el pueblo trabajan conjuntamente como participante/espectador para asegurar el beneficio colectivo e individual.

En los objetos de arte popular ceremonial, los simbolos determinan las formas. Los aspectos profundamente religiosos se expresan en los Trajes de las Danzas, en las Máscaras, en Incensarios y Candelabros, en los conceptos del Cielo y el Infierno, en las figuras del Dia de Muertos. Tambien son una de las formas de representar un Calendario Anual de Fiestas, profundamente enraizado en el Ciclo Agricola del Maiz, y de los Santos que sustituyeron a los antiguos Dioses a quien le reza uno para la protección de la familia y el éxito en las cosechas.

Huichols—From Ritual to Market
The Huichol, a people of the Western Sierra Madre of Nayarit, Jalisco, Zacatecas and Durango, had been isolated for centuries by rugged mountains. Their culture and beliefs remained intact, and their mythological view of history and life cycles were transmitted by shamans through an extensive oral tradition combined with peyote rituals, chanting, storytelling, ceremonies and festivities. Their rituals, ceremonies and lifestyle encompass a wealth of symbols, objects and traditional arts. Since the early 20th century anthropologists have been fascinated by the Huichol, and with the advent of road building, missionaries, government programs in the 1950s, and seasonal work migration, the Huichol's world has been brought to market. Many urban Huichol are now producing more marketable versions of their sacred prayer bowls, *ojos de Dios*, prayer arrows, yarn and bead work, and ritual masks.

Plate 52
Cresencio Perez Robles, *La Guirapa*, Huichol yarn painting, ca 1972, 23 1/2 x 23 1/2 inches.

Plate 53
Cresencio Perez Robles, *Goddess of the Deer*, Huichol yarn painting, ca. 1972, 23 1/2 x 23 1/2 inches.

Plate 54
Huichol hats, Shaman's chair, stool (Sierra de Nayarit), ca 1970.
These men's hats are part of an elaborate costume that includes game bags, beaded jewelry, belts and embroidered pants and shirt. The hats are made of woven straw and are ornamented with a red wool cross, beaded, woven or embroidered hatbands, and brims that are hung with *madrona* leaves, seed pods, beaded crosses, hawk or irridescent bird feathers, paper or other representations of leaves.

Plate 55 (top)
Huichol Offering Bowls
5 inches (d.) x 2 1/4 (approx.).
Predecessor to yarn paintings (left), these decorated bowls were made from hollowed out gourds which were coated with beeswax. The yarn pictures were then added. The bowls are used as offerings to the old grandfather fire god *Tatewary*. Beaded bowl (right) contains an eagle design, a deer, a cross, eye of god, prayer arrow, sun and other designs.

Plate 56 (bottom)
Beaded Bowl, hollowed out gourd, beeswax and beads. Made for tourist market by Huichol Indians.

Plate 57 (top)
Huichol Painted and Beaded Masks. Painted wooden mask (left); beaded wooden mask (right). Huichol Indians, ca. 1970. The painted mask pre-dates the beaded mask. Both masks depict Huichol symbols for the *Eye of God*, the sacred *Maize*, and the sacred *Deer*. Both are made for tourist trade.

Plate 58 (bottom)
Incense/candle holders, earthenware: large cow and rider; small deer; small cow,. On loan from Eleanor and Gary Gossen. *Candle holder* (cow with rider). On loan from Annie O'Neill.

Day of the Dead

Each year dead souls return to earth to celebrate with friends and family, and each year *El Día de los Muertos* is celebrated with renewed faith and energy. The festivities begin the afternoon of October 31st when the *angelitos* (children who have died) start arriving, in time for All Saints Day on November 1st. November 2nd (All Souls Day) is devoted to deceased adults. Extensive preparations are made for their return: elaborate altars with foods and offerings are created, grave sites are decorated with gorgeous wreathes and flowers, and in many villages, marigold petals are scattered along paths from the graves to the altars so the dead souls can find their way. Sweet offerings are just a small part of the culinary delights placed on an altar to tempt the returning souls. After feasting on the smells of *mole*, tastes of *tamales*, and swigs of beer, it might be time to indulge a sweet tooth.

Two weeks before the holiday, markets are filled with handmade objects devoted to death. The imagery is wild and animated, satiric and humorous and include sugar skulls and ceramic and wooden skeletons from all walks of life, engaged in all mortal activities.

El Dia de Muertos
Cada año regresan las almas de los muertos a la tierra para celebrar con amigos y familiares, y cada año el Dia de Muertos es celebrado con renovada fé y energía. Las fiestas comienzan la tarde del 31 de octubre cuando llegan los angelitos (niños que han muerto), para estar a tiempo para Todos Santos el 1ro de Noviembre. El dos de noviembre, Santos Difuntos, es dedicado a los adultos que han muerto. Exhaustivos preparativos se realizan para preparar su regreso: en las casas se montan altares muy elaborados con comida y ofrendas. Las tumbas son decoradas con preciosas guirnaldas y flores, y en muchos pueblos, pétalos de cempaxùchitl señalan la ruta de la tumba al altar para que el alma de los muertos encuentre su camino. Ofrendas de dulce son sólo una pequeña muestra de las delicias culinarias colocadas en un altar para atraer a las almas que retornan. Después del festín absorbiendo el olor y esencia del mole, los tamales y algunos tragos de cerveza, es hora de mimarse con unos dulcecitos.

Dos semanas antes de la fiesta, los mercados se llenan de objetos artesanales con figuras de calaveras. Las imágenes son caprichosas y vigorosas, satírica y cómica, e incluyen calaveras de azùcar, y esqueletos de barro y madera representando todas las actividades mortales de todos los personajes vivos.

Plate 59
Miguel Linares, *Skelton Street Vendor*
Mexico, D.F., mid 1970s,
paper, wood, wire and paint
In bygone days an astonishing array of vendors sold their wares in the streets of Mexico City where a cacophony could be heard from daybreak to sundown. The great Mexican graphic artist Posada portrayed these vendors as skeletons in a series of satiric broadsides dedicated to men and women at work. This *señor* represents a seller of papier-mâché Judas figures traditionally sold during Holy Week. The custom of making these brightly painted figures of devils, bandits, evil politicians and other nefarious types is still alive, but it is rare for people to gather together to see the Judas figures extinguished by burning—a symbolic destruction of evil.

Heaven and Hell

Under the Holy Inquisition's watchful eye, right in the atrium of churches, the clergy created ritual theater to further their evangelization labor. Reenactments of Mary and Joseph's ordeal during Christmas led to the *Pastorela*, and the *Via Crucis* during Holy Week to a *Passion Play*. The terror the Friars tried to transmit about Heaven and Hell was greatly modified and toned down in Mexican culture: devils were depicted with particular zeal and humor, while angels took on the childlike physical attributes as cherubs. Children who died unchristened were likened to them.

Dances tolerated by the Church were performed during these festivities, and certain characters in red masks were incorporated. According to Father Sahagún, a 16th century chronicler, festivities that took place prior to the Spanish Invasion in September and March were dedicated to the god *Tezcatlipoca* (Smoking Mirror) whose body was painted half red and half black. As late as 1755 the Inquisition suspected paganism was underlying some rituals and prohibited them. During the second half of the 19th century, the *Fiesta* processions, dances and plays were performed in the streets and public open spaces in a clear move to reappropriate century old traditions.

Cielo E Infierno

Baja la mirada severa de la Santa Inquisición, en los atrios de las iglesias, el clero creó un teatro ritual para ampliar su labor evangelizadora. El Nacimiento de Cristo y las peripecias de María y José derivaron en la creación de la *Pastorela*, y el *Via Crucis* durante la Semana Santa se conoce por *La Pasión de Cristo*. El terror que los frailes trataron de imponer sobre El Cielo y el Infierno fue modificado y atenuado en la Cultura Mexicana: los diablos se convirtieron en traviesos y sagaces personajes, los angeles tomaron la cachondez de los querubines, al grado que los niños que mueren sin bautizarse son llamados *angelitos*.

Danzas toleradas por la Iglesia eran realizadas durante estas festividades, y ciertos personajes con máscaras rojas se incorporaron. Según el padre Sahagún, un cronista del siglo XVI, las festividades que se efectuaban previas a la Invasion en los meses de Septiembre y Marzo estaban dedicadas al dios *Tezcatlipoca* (o Espejo de Obsidiana), cuyo cuerpo y rostro estaban pintados mitad rojo y mitad negro. Todavía en 1755 la Santa Inquisición sospechaba de prácticas paganas detrás de algunas de estas danzas y máscaras y las prohibió. Durante la segunda mitad del siglo XIX, las procesiones, danzas y representaciones de teatro ritual dentro de las Fiesta tomaron las calles, cerros y espacios públicos en un movimiento claro de reapropiación de tradiciones centenarias.

Plate 60 and 61
Day of the Dead Installation View, University Art Museum, 1992. Photograph (Patampan, Michoacán, 1976) used for mural by Annie O'Neill. Mural by Neil McGreevy Studios, Albany, New York.

Ocumicho, Michoacán

Many years ago artisans in the Tarascan village of Ocumicho made large pottery water storage vessels and seasonally sculpted clay whistles and banks for sale at fiestas and special markets. In 1966 the innovative young creator of Ocumicho devils died. His clients went to **Teodoro Martinez Benito** and his wife, **Maria Guadalupe Alvarez Sanchez**, to make these odd pieces and although Teodoro was a wood carver the couple began to produce stranger and more grotesque pieces. As they acquired an international following more and more farmers and seasonal artisans turned to ceramics. Ocumicho is now known for its unbridled boldness of expression. Their work is stylistically faddish and easily influenced by outside demands. Subjects range from devils and grotesque interpretations of hell, to Last Supper watermelon feasts, to macabre *Day of the Dead* sculptures. All the traditional icons and symbols are irreverently portrayed in vividly painted and varnished tableau. Pottery that was traditionally made by woman is now a family operation. The success of these potters in the late 1960s coincided with the height of government subsidy of popular pottery for internal and foreign markets.

Plate 62
Day of the Dead Breadmaking Activity
Ocumicho, Michoacán, 1978, single-fired, painted, and varnished earthenware, 7 3/4 x 9 x 2 inches (average size figure); Devil Oven, 12 3/4 x 7 x 10 inches,
Ocumichu Indians have a repertoire of figural ceramics which includes bizarre devils, wild and macabre *Day of the Dead* figures (pictured here) and other ceremonial tableau depictions which are uninhibited and primitive, making them prized possessions of collectors.

Plate 63
Last Supper (Ocumicho, Michoacán), ca. 1970, single-fired, painted and varnished earthenware 14 x 11 x 9 inches.

Plate 64 (catalog cover)
Selected Figures from Heaven and Hell Installation, University Art Museum, 1992.
Wooden devils and bull by Manuel Jiménez

83

Acknowledgments

First and foremost I am indebted to Annie O'Neill for the large number of pieces from her collection that she has contributed to the exhibition, and also for the informative text which accompanies the catalog photographs. She has generously shared the fruits of her long-held passion for Mexican folk art as collector, advisor, folklorist, artist, and now friend. Whether one is a devoted University Art Museum viewer or first-time visitor, the experience of encountering even a small portion of this extraordinary collection is an intoxicating assault on the senses. Her enthusiasm for each and every object in her collection is infectious and choosing what to bring to the museum and what to leave behind was difficult. Choices were made easier with the addition to the team of Marta Turok, an anthropologist from Mexico who specializes in popular culture. A recognized champion of that country's artisans, her input helped to focus the exhibit and gave it flight.

At each meeting with Annie we explored ways to focus the exhibit and discussed reasons for accepting or rejecting a particular object, based on Marta's interpretation of *Culture in Transition* and Annie's willingness to lend or not (which was more *lend* than not!). It was a curatorial and personal growth experience and I thank them both *con un gran fuerte abrazo*.

I am also sincerely grateful to Mr. and Mrs. Eugene Walter, who lent from their extraordinary collection of Mexican masks, and to Pilar Gomez who lent costumes used for the dances of the *Concheras*, *Negritos*, *Quetzales*, *Matachines*, *Viejitos* and *Chinelos*. Other individual lenders are cited elsewhere in the catalog contents and I thank them for their generosity.

In addition, I want to thank Dr. Gary Gossen, Director of the Mesoamerican Institute at the University at Albany, who wisely pointed me in Marta's direction. I am also grateful to Eleanor Gossen of the University Libraries for her research assistance and open door policy for guests from Mexico. Annie O'Neill's parents, Dorothy and Seon Felshin were also gracious hosts to our museum staff.

Every exhibition—from its beginning stages to the final museum installation—depends upon the support, hard work and cooperation of many people. I especially want to express my appreciation for the early interest in and support for the project by H. Patrick Swygert, President of the University at Albany, and the helpfulness of his assistant, Sheila Mahan. Important support was also given by the Honorable Manuel Alonso, Consul General of Mexico, and Mireya Terán, Executive Director of the Mexican Cultural Institute of New York. All of them made frequent visits during the installation process with words of encouragement and delight that were much appreciated by the installation crew, not to mention the curators.

The most hard-working member of the crew was Zheng Hu, the museum designer, who visually interpreted the curators' installation concept with a brilliance and sensitivity now enjoyed daily by visitors to the exhibition. Marta Turok had the best description of our collaboration with Zheng: *Oriental cleanliness of line meets Mexican baroque!* No visual detail was too small or insignificant to escape his attention. The lovely and intelligent design for the exhibition catalog is also his creation.

I was happy to have had the assistance on the project of Joanne Lue, the museum secretary and co-editor of the catalog. As usual, her considerable skill, good humor and willingness to work ten days

a week enabled the voluminous (bilingual!) catalog and label text to get done, on top of the general on-going museum business and correspondence. She was always there for the staff, lenders, and sponsors.

Many others deserve recognition and thanks. Gary Gold, the catalog photographer, consistently stayed with the project not knowing if we would ever be able to offer remuneration. Neil McGreevy, another photographer, did the beautiful murals used in the installation design. Graduate assistants Andrew Boardman, D. Alex Dunwoodie, Ming Lu and Ivelina Ramagosa, and volunteers Joseph Lue, Jr., Josh Rozett, James Wallin and Norman Bauman—all worked long into many nights. The sponsors of the exhibition itself, cited elsewhere in the catalog, made many aspects possible. The Capital Region members of the *Friends of Mexico Committee* helped with fundraising efforts. Edna Acosta-Belen and other members of the University's Latin American and Carribean Studies Department were also supportive with encouragement and advice as was David Gonzalez of the Hispanic Heritage Institute. And I am *most* grateful to the *Fideicomiso para la Cultura Mexico-Estados Unidos* and the *Office of the President, University at Albany*, who made the publication of this catalog possible.

Finally and most especially, I would like to thank Nancy Liddle, soon to be *Director Emeritus* of the museum. Her belief in my abilities and her encouragement of my professional development over the many years of our association prepared me to undertake this project successfully.

Marijo Dougherty
Project Director

Installation photographs by Joanne Lue

LENDERS TO THE EXHIBITION

Annie O'Neill, New Paltz, New York

Marta Turok, Mexico City, Mexico

Pilar Gomez, New York, New York

Mr. and Mrs. Eugene J. Walter, Norwood, New Jersey

Cullen and Shirley Burris, Schenectady, New York

Nina Felshin, New York, New York

Eleanor and Gary Gossen, Albany, New York

Mr. and Mrs. James Wilson, Schenectady, New York

MAJOR SPONSORS OF THE EXHIBITION

Community Health Plan/CHP

Office of the President, University at Albany

Mexican Cultural Institute of New York

University Auxiliary Services at Albany, Inc.

Irving and Elaine Kirsch

Selected works from the exhibition will be shown at the SUNY Plattsburgh Art Museum, Plattsburgh, New York, February 27 through April 11, 1993.